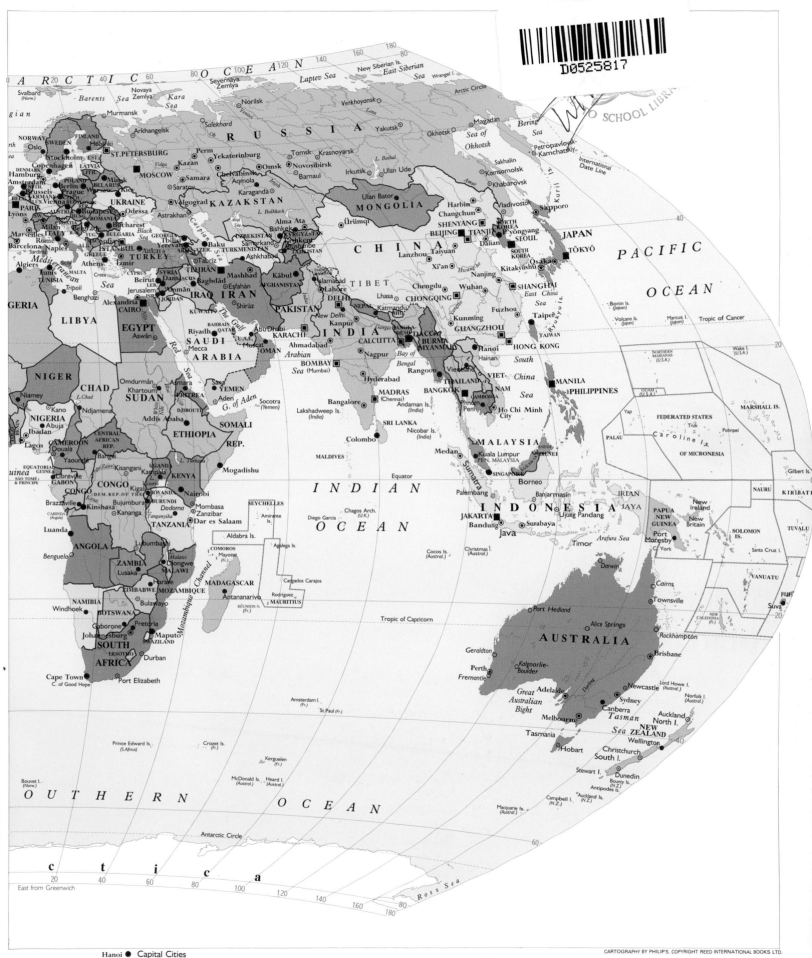

/911

ARCTIC OCEAN

Svalbard (Norw.)

Novaya Zemlya

Barents Sea

Kara Sea

Severnaya Zemlya

Laptev Sea

New Siberian Is. East Siberian Sea

Wrangel I.

Arctic Circle

Murmansk

Norilsk

Verkhoyansk

Magadan

Bering Sea

60

NORWAY SWEDEN FINLAND

Salekhard

Ob

Yenisey

Lena

Okhotsk

Sea of Okhotsk

Petropavlovsk-Kamchatskiy

Oslo Helsinki

Arkhangelsk

Tomsk Krasnoyarsk

Yakutsk

International Date Line

STOCKHOLM EST.

ST.PETERSBURG

Perm Yekaterinburg

Omsk Novosibirsk

Irkutsk Ulan Ude

L. Baikal

Sakhalin

Komsomolsk

Sapporo

Copenhagen DENMARK LATVIA LITH.

Volga

MOSCOW

Kazan

Chelyabinsk

Barnaul

Amur

Khabarovsk

Vladivostok

Kuril Is.

40

Hamburg NETH. POLAND BELARUS

Samara

Karaganda

Ulan Bator

Harbin

NORTH KOREA

Amsterdam GERMANY Berlin

Kiev

Saratov

Aqmola

MONGOLIA

Changchun

SHENYANG

BEIJING TIANJIN P'yongyang

Brussels LUX. Vienna CZECH. UKRAINE

Volgograd

KAZAKSTAN

L. Balkhash

Dalian

SEOUL

JAPAN

PARIS AUSTRIA Budapest ROMANIA

Odessa

Astrakhan

Aral Sea

Alma Ata

SOUTH KOREA

Osaka

TŌKYŌ

Lyons SW. ITALY Belgrade CROATIA BULGARIA

Black Sea

GEORGIA

Caspian Sea

Bishkek UZBEKISTAN KYRGYZSTAN

Ürümqi

Kitakyūshū

PACIFIC

Marseilles Rome Naples ALB.

Tbilisi

Baku

Samarkand Tashkent

CHINA

OCEAN

Barcelona Sardinia GREECE ISTANBUL

Sofia

ARM. AZER. TURKMENISTAN

Dushanbe TAJIKISTAN

Lanzhou Taiyuan

Xi'an

Hwang Ho

Algiers Tunis MALTA Crete

Athens Izmir

TURKEY

Yerevan Ankara

Ashkhabad

Mashhad

Kābul

Lhasa

Chengdu

Nanjing

SHANGHAI

Mediterranean Sea

CYPRUS SYRIA TEHRĀN

Tabrīz

AFGHANISTAN Islamabad

TIBET

CHONGQING

Wuhan

East China Sea

Benghazi

Beirut LEB. Damascus Baghdād

Esfahān

Lahore

DELHI

Kanpur

Kunming

GUANGZHOU

Fuzhou

Taipei

Alexandria Jerusalem ISR. Ammān IRAQ IRAN

New Delhi

NEPAL Katmandu

TAIWAN

CAIRO JORDAN

KUWAIT

PAKISTAN

Ganges

BANGLA-DESH DACCA

HONG KONG

LIBYA

EGYPT

Riyadh QATAR BAHRAIN

Abu Dhabi

Karachi

Ahmadabad

INDIA

CALCUTTA

BURMA MIYANMAR

Hanoi

Hainan

South China Sea

NIGER

CHAD

SUDAN

Omdurmân Khartoum

Asmara ERITREA

SANA' YEMEN

Mecca U.A.E. Muscat OMAN

Aswân

Red Sea

Arabian Sea

Nagpur

BOMBAY (Mumbai)

Bay of Bengal

Rangoon

Vientiane

VIET-NAM

MANILA

Niamey L.Chad Ndjamena

Kano Abuja

SAUDI ARABIA

Hyderabad

MADRAS (Chennai)

Andaman Is. (India)

THAILAND

BANGKOK

CAMBODIA

Phnom Penh

PHILIPPINES

FEDERATED STATES

NIGERIA

Ibadan Lagos

Addis Ababa

G. of Aden

DJIBOUTI

Aden

Socotra (Yemen)

Bangalore

Lakshadweep Is. (India)

SRI LANKA

Nicobar Is. (India)

Ho Chi Minh City

GUAM (U.S.A.)

Yap

OF MICRONESIA

Truk

Caroline Is.

Pohnpei

MARSHALL IS.

CAMEROON Douala Yaoundé

ETHIOPIA

SOMALI REP.

Colombo

MALDIVES

Medan

MALAYSIA

SABAH

PALAU

Gilbert Is.

EQUATORIAL GUINEA

SÃO TOMÉ & PRÍNCIPE

GABON Libreville

CENTRAL AFRICAN REP.

Bangui

Kisangani

UGANDA Kampala

Congo (Zaire)

KENYA

L. Turkana

Mogadishu

Equator

INDIAN

Kuala Lumpur PEN. MALAYSIA

SINGAPORE

BRUNEI

Borneo

IRIAN

NAURU

KIRIBATI

Brazzaville Kinshasa

CONGO DEM. REP. OF THE

Kasai

RWANDA Kigali BURUNDI Bujumbura

L. Victoria

Nairobi

Dodoma

Mombasa

SEYCHELLES

Amirante Is.

Diego Garcia

Chagos Arch. (U.K.)

OCEAN

Palembang

JAKARTA

Bandung

Banjarmasin

Surabaya

INDONESIA

Ujung Pandang

JAYA

PAPUA NEW GUINEA

New Ireland

New Britain

SOLOMON IS.

TUVALU

Luanda

ANGOLA

CABINDA (Angola)

Kananga

L. Tanganyika

TANZANIA

Zanzibar

Dar es Salaam

Aldabra Is.

Agalega Is.

Cocos Is. (Austral.)

Christmas I. (Austral.)

Java

Timor

Arafura Sea

Port Moresby

C. York

Darwin

NEW CALEDONIA (Fr.)

VANUATU

Benguela

Lubumbashi

L. Malawi

COMOROS

Mayotte (Fr.)

Cargados Carajos

Santa Cruz Is.

FIJI

ZAMBIA

Lusaka

MALAWI Lilongwe

MADAGASCAR

Rodriguez (Fr.)

Tropic of Capricorn

Port Hedland

Alice Springs

Cairns

Townsville

Suva

NAMIBIA

ZIMBABWE Harare

Bulawayo

MOZAMBIQUE

Antananarivo

RÉUNION (Fr.) MAURITIUS

AUSTRALIA

Rockhampton

Windhoek

BOTSWANA

Gaborone Pretoria

Mozambique Channel

Amsterdam I. (Fr.)

St. Paul (Fr.)

Geraldton

Perth Fremantle

Kalgoorlie-Boulder

Great Australian Bight

Brisbane

Lord Howe I. (Austral.)

Norfolk I. (Austral.)

Johannesburg Maputo

SOUTH AFRICA

LESOTHO SWAZILAND

Durban

Adelaide

Newcastle

Sydney

Canberra

Auckland North I.

Cape Town C. of Good Hope

Port Elizabeth

Prince Edward Is. (S.Africa)

Crozet Is. (Fr.)

Kerguelen (Fr.)

McDonald Is. (Austral.) Heard I. (Austral.)

Melbourne

Tasmania

Murray

Hobart

Tasman Sea

NEW ZEALAND

Christchurch

South I.

Stewart I.

Campbell Is. (N.Z.)

Macquarie Is. (Austral.)

Wellington

Dunedin

Bounty Is. (N.Z.)

Antipodes Is. (N.Z.)

Auckland Is. (N.Z.)

SOUTHERN OCEAN

Antarctic Circle

ctica

East from Greenwich

Ross Sea

Hanoi ● Capital Cities

PHILIP'S

HISTORY ATLAS

Published in Great Britain by
George Philip Ltd,
an imprint of Reed Consumer Books Ltd,
Michelin House,
81 Fulham Road,
London SW3 6RB
and Aukland and Melbourne

Copyright © 1998 George Philip

ISBN 0-540-07602-3

A CIP catalogue record for this book is available
from the British Library

Printed in China

Editor Jane Edmonds

Assistant editor Jannet King

Cartography by Philip's Map Studio

Additional cartography by Cosmographics, Watford

Cartographic editor Hazell Lintott

Designed by The Design Revolution, Brighton

Picture Credits Front cover
Elizabeth I: Bridgeman Art Library (Philip Mould, Historical Portraits,
London)
Nelson Mandela: Rex Features (Frederick de Klerk)

The map of trench warfare on page 41 is based on a map in
The Atlas of the First World War by Martin Gilbert (1970),
by permission of Routledge

CONTENTS

THE ROMAN EMPIRE

The Defence of the Empire AD 100–300

- —— Imperial frontier AD 106
- ● Important provincial capital
- Territory occupied after AD 106
- ⊏⊐ Defence works
- ⊏⊐ African fortifications
- —— Main Roman road
- —·— Boundary between the Eastern and Western Empire 3rd century AD
- ⊠ Legionary base
- ↓ Naval base

In establishing a great empire, which at its peak stretched from Britain in the northwest to Syria in the east, the Romans helped to lay the foundations of European civilisation. Wherever the Roman army established control, science was employed for practical ends, from underfloor heating and watermills, to aqueducts and an impressive road network. The Romans introduced an efficient system of government and a language that was understood everywhere. They also adopted and spread Christianity.

▼ Rome controlled the entire Italian peninsula by 275 BC. It then embarked on a long campaign of conquest, defeating the Carthaginians and Greeks before expanding into northern Europe and Asia.

▲ The Romans defended the frontiers of their empire by building many forts, wooden palisades and walls.

The Roman Empire at its Peak AD 106

- —— Imperial frontier AD 106
- Roman expansion to 201 BC
- Roman expansion 201–100 BC
- Roman expansion 100–44 BC
- Roman expansion 44 BC–AD 14
- Roman expansion AD 14–96
- Roman expansion AD 96–106
- GAL Roman province
- *Agri* Roman region
- ● Roman provincial capital

► In AD 410 Rome was sacked by the Visigoths, signalling the end of the Western half of the empire. However, the Eastern half was to continue as the Byzantine Empire until 1453.

Invasions and Migrations AD 375–450

▨ Gothic territory before c. 375	→ Goths
▨ Hun territory before c. 375	→ Visigoths
▬·▬ Roman imperial frontier 395	→ Sarmatians and others
✕ Battle	→ Vandals
Movements of peoples with approximate date:	→ Burgundians
→ Huns	→ Sueves
→ Alans	Anglo–Saxons

North Sea
Baltic Sea
from 410
from 410
ANGLO–SAXONS
London
BURGUNDIANS 410
375–405 ALANS 375
HUNS 375 Volga
Rhine
Dnieper
Dniester
Don
HUNS 405
GOTHS
376
Bordeaux 418
412
SUEVES 410
411
VISIGOTHS
378 SARMATIANS 377
Black Sea
Tarragona
Rome
Adriatic Sea
408–10
Danube
375–78
VISIGOTHS
Constantinople
Tingis 429
Mediterranean Sea
Carthage 439
ALANS
VANDALS
Corinth
Aegean Sea
395
Hadrianople 378
Antioch
395
395

Trade in the Roman Empire

Items of trade:
- ◊ oil
- ⊛ metals
- ◉ grain
- ▼ wine
- ✦ fish
- ◈ slaves
- ▼ marble
- ▮ ceramics
- △ amber
- —— Imperial frontier AD 106
- --- Main trade route

50°
Londinium
50°
Massilia
Sirmium
Gades
Corsica
Sardinia
Roma
Byzantium
Sicily
Crete
Antiochia
Cyprus
Carthago
Damascus
Cyrene
Alexandria
40°
30°
0° 10° 20° 30° 40°

Pontus Euxinus
MOESIA INFERIOR
THRACIA
BITHYNIA AND PONTUS
ASIA
Ancyra
GALATIA
CAPPADOCIA
LYCIA AND PAMPHYLIA
CILICIA
Antiochia
SYRIA
CYPRUS
...ostrum
Alexandria
JUDAEA
ARABIA
AEGYPTUS

▲ Trade was very important in the Roman Empire. To feed the many people in the towns, corn was imported first from Sicily, later from Africa. Luxury goods such as silk, ivory, and hair for wigs, were imported from China, Africa and Germany.

5

ROMAN BRITAIN

A Roman army first invaded Britain in 55 and 54 BC, under the leadership of Julius Caesar. It withdrew after defeating a number of tribes, including the Catuvellauni and Trinovantes, but these tribes continued to pose a threat to the Romans across the English Channel in Gaul. The Romans were also aware that Britain contained many valuable resources, such as tin and iron. Consequently, in AD 43 Emperor Claudius launched a full-scale expedition. The Roman legions experienced only occasional difficulty in dealing with the forces that opposed them, and by AD 60 they controlled England as far north as the River Humber, and by 80 the whole of Wales. The new governor, Agricola, then pushed northwards into Scotland. The Romans found it hard to maintain a presence in Scotland, but they ruled the southern half of Britain for almost 400 years. Much of England became a peaceful province in which many adopted the Roman way of life.

Roman Campaigns in the North AD 69–84

- **SEL** Name of tribe
- ○ Roman settlement
- → Roman campaigns AD 69–74
- → Roman campaigns under Agricola AD 79–84
- ✕ Possible site of Battle of Mons Graupius AD 83
- ✿ Conquest of area or people

The Roman Conquest of Southern Britain AD 43–61

- **SIL** Name of tribe
- ⌂ Hill fort
- ○ Roman settlement (present-day name in brackets)
- → Roman campaigns AD 43–47
- → Roman campaigns AD 48–60
- → Movements of Boudicca's Iceni army AD 60–61
- ✕ Battle
- ✿ Conquest of area or people

▲ Agricola, the Roman governor of Britain between AD 78 and 85, was convinced of the need to conquer Scotland. In 83 he won a great victory over the Caledonians at the Battle of Mons Graupius, thus gaining the whole of lowland Scotland for the empire. The gain, however, was only temporary.

◄ The Roman invasion force in AD 43 consisted of 40,000 men. They marched through southeast England and captured the town of Camulodunum, from where they advanced to the Severn and Trent rivers. They only met with serious resistance when they reached Wales, where Caractacus led the opposing forces until his defeat in 51. By 60 the Romans controlled England as far north as the Humber, but in that year Boudicca, Queen of the Iceni, led a major revolt. The greater armed power of the Romans eventually prevailed, and secured a crushing victory over Boudicca in 61.

Invasions in the 4th and 5th Centuries AD

Routes of:
→ Angles
→ Saxons
→ Jutes
→ Scots, Irish and Picts
⊠ Roman legionary base
○ Roman town

PICTS

SCOTS

HIBERNIA

IRISH

Eburacum
(York)

Lindum
(Lincoln)

Deva
(Chester)

Glevum
(Gloucester)

Camulodunum
(Colchester)

Isca
(Caerleon)

Londinium
(London)

Dubris
(Dover)

GAUL

Roman Britain in the 2nd–4th Centuries AD

— Roman road
○ Roman town
⊠ Roman legionary base
▫ Roman fort

Antonine Wall
(built AD 140-42)

Trimontium
(Newstead)

DERE STREET

Hadrian's Wall
(built AD 122-36)

(High Rochester)

Segedunum
(Wallsend)

Luguvallium
(Carlisle)

Corstopitum
(Corbridge)

(Chester-
le-Street)

(Maryport)

(Kirkby
Thore)

Vinovia
(Binchester)

(Bowes)

Veterae
(Brough)

Cataractonium
(Catterick)

(Lancaster)

Isurium
(Aldborough)

Eburacum
(York)

Oceanus Hibernicus
(Irish Sea)

(Ilkley)

(Tadcaster)

Oceanus Germanicus
(North Sea)

Mancunium
(Manchester)

(Doncaster)

ERMINE STREET

Lindum
(Lincoln)

Canovium
(Caerhun)

Deva
(Chester)

Segontium
(Caernarfon)

(Ancaster)

Viroconium
(Wroxeter)

WATLING STREET

Ratae
(Leicester)

(Brancaster)

Venta Icenorum
(Caistor)

Gariannonum
(Burgh Castle)

Venonae
(High Cross)

(Castor)

Magnis
(Kenchester)

WAY

(BRITISH) WAY

(Walton Castle)

Moridunum
(Carmarthen)

Glevum
(Gloucester)

(Dunstable)

ICKNIELD

Camulodunum
(Colchester)

(Abergavenny)

Venta Silurum
(Caerwent)

(Cirencester)

Verulamium
(St Albans)

Othona
(Bradwell)

Isca
(Caerleon)

FOSSE

Londinium
(London)

(Reculver)

Aquae Sulis
(Bath)

Calleva
Atrebatum
(Silchester)

(Rochester)

Rutupiae
(Richborough)

(Ilchester)

Venta Belgarum
(Winchester)

(Canterbury)

Sorviodunum
(Old Sarum)

(Portchester)

(Lympne)

Dubris
(Dover)

Isca Dumnoniorum
(Exeter)

(Dorchester)

Noviomagus
(Chichester)

Anderida
(Pevensey)

Oceanus Britannicus
(English Channel)

▲ In the 4th century AD Saxon raiders began to attack the southeast coast. At the same time Picts and Scots threatened the northern frontier, destroying Hadrian's Wall and overrunning much of the north in 367. Shortly afterwards the Roman forces began to withdraw, and by the early 5th century they had abandoned Britain.

◄ In an effort to secure their position in the north, the Romans built Hadrian's Wall in the 120s. Twenty years later they attempted to subdue Scotland and built the Antonine Wall, but by 200 Hadrian's Wall again formed the northern frontier. To the south Britain was divided, in the early 3rd century, into two provinces: Britannia Superior and Britannia Inferior, of which Londinium and Eburacum were the capitals. Londinium was at the centre of a road network which not only encouraged trade but also enabled Roman troops to march quickly to any region where they were needed to keep the local population under control.

ANCIENT AND MEDIEVAL CHINA

In the 2nd millennium BC large parts of northern China were conquered and ruled by the Shang Dynasty, followed by the Zhou. By the 5th century BC, however, seven major states were competing for control of China. Between 280 and 221 BC the state of Qin eventually achieved supremacy over the others, and King Zheng proclaimed himself 'First Emperor'. His early death provided the Hans with an opportunity to establish a dynasty which was to rule China for over 400 years. During this time China had a population of over 50 million, which was often mobilised for warfare and large public works. Walled cities became the focal points of a trading network that stretched across the empire. A series of peasant revolts hastened the collapse of the Han Empire in AD 220, and it was not until 624 that China was reunited by the Tang Dynasty, ushering in a golden age of expansion and prosperity. The end of the dynasty in 907 heralded another period of disunity until the Song Dynasty was established in 960. The empire over which the Song ruled was constantly under threat from the non-Chinese people to the north, but it survived until 1276 when the whole of China fell to the Mongols.

The Qin and Han Empires

—— Extent of Qin and Han Empires 206 BC	⌇⌇⌇ Great Wall
—— Territory added to Han Empire by AD 23	AD 23 Date at which area subjugated
- - - Further territory added to Han Empire by AD 210	→ Major campaign
—— Western regions under Han Protectorate	*XIO* Name of people

▲ Both the Qin and Han emperors were determined to expand the frontiers of the lands over which they ruled. They were also determined to keep the nomadic non-Chinese out of the empire, and in the 3rd century BC the Qin emperor joined sections of existing walled defences to create the Great Wall.

East and Central Asia 624–907

—— Tang Empire 624–907	
⧄ Chinese cultural region outside empire	
—— Area under Tang control 645–763	
—— Tang military protectorate 659–65	
SILL Name of people	
—— Eastern boundary of the Abbasid Empire c. 750	
✕ Battle	

China under the Northern Song c. 1000

▨ Boundary of Song China	── Major navigable river
⊠ Major trading centre	┈┈ Canal
⊠ Other trading centre	── Boundary of administrative region
── Main trade route	**TAN** People

◄ The Chinese Empire over which the Song ruled did not include Central Asia, and on its northern border it faced the hostile states of Liao and Xixia. However, the Song period saw a revival in the native Chinese philosophy of Confucianism. The number of scholar-officials greatly increased, with 400,000 candidates sitting exams each year. Scholarly families fuelled a demand for books, and there were many improvements in printing, including the use of moveable type. New forms of art also flourished with the encouragement of the emperor. Emperor Huizong (r. 1100–26) was blamed for the loss of the north to Jurchen invaders because he allowed his interest in art to distract him from government.

▼ The Song lost the north to a confederation of Jurchen tribes from the mountains of east Siberia in 1127. They then moved their capital from Kaifeng (at the centre of the canal and road network) to Hangzhou. The Jurchen, who established the Jin Dynasty, adopted Kaifeng as their capital in 1161.

◄ The influence of the Tang Dynasty was felt throughout Asia for almost 300 years. The trade routes of the Silk Road were brought under China's control, and by the mid-7th century the Chinese Empire had reached its greatest extent prior to the conquests of the Manchus 1000 years later. However, in 751 two major defeats were inflicted on the Tang – one by the Arabs at the Battle of Talas River and the other by the Kingdom of Nanzhao at the Battle of Dali. From this point Tang influence began to wane.

East Asia in 1150

── Boundary of empire or kingdom c. 1150	
MON People	

RELIGION IN THE MEDIEVAL WORLD

The First Crusade 1095–99
- ∴ Main area of crusade recruitment
- + + Secondary area of crusade recruitment
- Latin Christendom
- *SEL* Muslim state
- Byzantine territory 1097
- --- Byzantine frontier 1070
- → Routes of main Crusader armies
- ⧄ Cilician Armenia

By the 11th century the Christian world consisted of much of Europe, while the Muslim world stretched from Persia in the east to Spain in the west. It included the Holy Land (Palestine) which, towards the end of the century, the Christians in Western Europe became intent on recapturing. In 1095 Pope Urban II launched the First Crusade and an expedition of perhaps 100,000 people set out for the Holy Land with the aim of seizing Jerusalem. This they succeeded in doing in 1099, after a month's siege, largely because the Muslims were so divided. However, over the next 200 years a further six major crusades and several minor ones had very mixed fortunes, and ultimately the Christians were unable to maintain control of Palestine. In 1292 the city of Acre, the last major crusader stronghold, fell to the Muslims.

▲ By the time the First Crusade reached Jersualem, it consisted of only 14,000 men. They managed, however, to capture the city and over the next 40 years to establish the boundaries of four crusader states.

The Crusader States 1186
- Byzantine Empire
- Cilician Armenia
- Crusader states
- Saladin's territories
- → Amalric's campaigns 1163-69
- ✕ Battle of Hattin
- ■ Hospitaller fortress
- □ Templar fortress

The Third Crusade 1189–92
- ‖ Routes of the main Crusader armies

▲ The arrival of the Third Crusade saved the crusader states from extinction by Saladin, a Kurd who had put an end to the Fatimid Caliphate based in Egypt.

► In the early 12th century the crusaders established the Kingdom of Jerusalem, the County of Tripoli, the Principality of Antioch and the County of Edessa. By 1186 they had lost Edessa.

▶ Participants in the Fourth Crusade of 1198–1204 were all from Latin Christian countries in Western Europe. They failed to reach Palestine, instead conquering Constantinople, the capital of the Orthodox Christian world. It was two orders of monastic knights – the Hospitallers of St John and the Knights Templar – who helped to ensure the survival of the crusader states. By the early 13th century the crusader states had reached their greatest extent, although they still covered little more than a coastal strip. The Fifth Crusade, with contingents from Germany, Italy, Austria, Hungary, England and France, came close to success in Egypt before its final defeat in 1221.

The Fifth Crusade 1217–21

☐ Venetian territories	▨ Gains in Outremer by 1240
SEL Muslim state	≣ Routes of main Crusader armies

▼ In the mid-13th century Islam came under attack from the 'pagan' Mongols, who conquered Central Asia and the area of present-day Iraq and Iran. However, in the same period Islam was permanently established in Anatolia and India, from where it spread to Southeast Asia. Here, Buddhism was the predominant religion, although there were small areas of Hinduism. Despite the influx of Muslims, and the establishment of the Sultanate of Delhi, Hinduism continued to be the main religion in India. Christianity became increasingly identified with Europe, although Christian minorities continued to exist in Egypt, the Middle East and Central Asia.

World Religions 750–1250

- Predominantly Christian 750
- Majority converted to Christianity 750–1250
- Predominantly Islamic 750
- Majority converted to Islam 750–1250
- Predominantly Buddhist 750
- Majority converted to Buddhism 750–1250
- Predominantly Hindu 750
- Judaism established religion
- China: Buddhism, Confucianism, Taoism
- Korea: Buddhism, Confucianism
- Manichaeism established religion
- Areas remaining to traditional religions

MEDIEVAL EUROPE

Between 950 and 1300 the population of Europe grew at such a pace that many new villages and towns were established and old towns were developed beyond their existing walls. Urban craftsmen produced an ever-increasing number of goods to sell in the new market-towns and farmers began to produce cash crops such as grain, grapes or wool. Regions started to specialise in, for example, the production of cloth or wine. At the same time, the Genoese and Venetians expanded their territories and gained control of trading routes throughout the Mediterranean Sea. It was via these routes that the Black Death first spread from Asia to Europe, reaching Genoa in January 1348. This pandemic of the bubonic plague went on to devastate most of Europe, resulting in the loss of perhaps a third of its population.

▶ In 1347 the bubonic plague reached the Crimean port of Caffa, from where a fleet of Genoese galleys carried it to Messina and then Genoa. Within four years it had swept through Europe, yet there were towns and regions that remained unaffected.

▶ In medieval Europe the wealth of many regions grew as a result of specialising in the production of particular crops or goods. By the beginning of the 12th century, for example, Flanders was the richest, most densely populated and urbanised region of northern Europe because it had specialised in producing cloth using wool from England. By the 13th century other areas of specialist production included the wine trade of Gascony, grain in Sicily, southern Italy and eastern Europe, timber and fish in Scandinavia and the Baltic, metal-working in the Rhineland, and cheese in eastern England, Holland and southern Poland.

The Economy of Medieval Europe

🐟 Fishing   🌲 Timber

Mining and panning:

△ salt   ⬣ pitch   ◨ copper   ◈ tin   ▲ wax   ▣ iron   ◆ lead

▣▣ silver (main and less important centres in 12th and 13th centuries)

Agricultural products:

◔ grain   🐎 horses   ✻ wine   ◉ olives   ◯ sugar   🐑 wool   ◕ cheese   ☘ dye plants   💧 olive oil

Manufactured goods:

✳ textiles   ◎ silk   ▨ leather   🗅 paper   ↖ metal wares

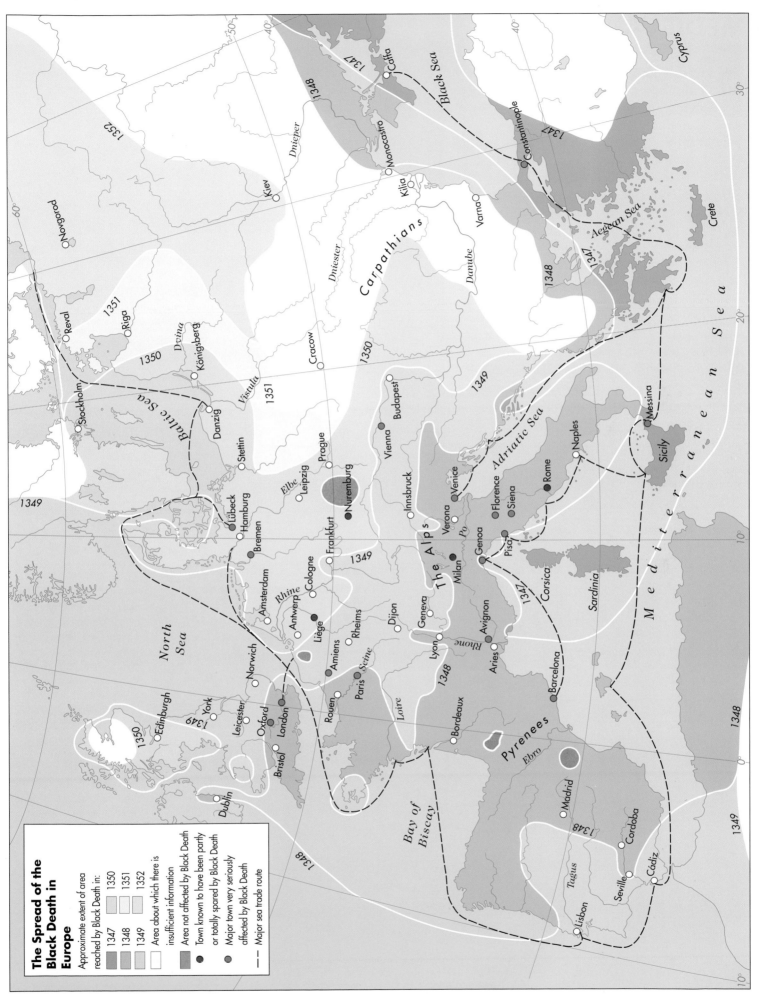

The Spread of the Black Death in Europe

Approximate extent of area reached by Black Death in:

1347	1350
1348	1351
1349	1352

Area about which there is insufficient information

Area not affected by Black Death

● Town known to have been partly or totally spared by Black Death

● Major town very seriously affected by Black Death

- - - Major sea trade route

Novgorod

Reval
Riga   1351
Königsberg   1350
Stockholm
Danzig
Stettin
Lübeck
Hamburg
Bremen
Amsterdam
Antwerp
Cologne
Liège
Amiens
Rouen
Paris
Rheims
Dijon
Norwich
Leicester
York
Oxford
London
Bristol
Dublin
Edinburgh

Kiev
Cracow
Prague
Leipzig
Frankfurt
Nuremburg
Budapest
Vienna
Innsbruck
Verona
Venice
Florence
Siena
Milan
Genoa
Pisa
Rome
Naples
Messina
Sicily
Avignon
Arles
Lyon
Geneva
Bordeaux
Barcelona
Madrid
Cordoba
Cadiz
Seville
Lisbon

Caffa
Monocastro
Kilia
Varna
Constantinople
Cyprus
Crete

North Sea
Baltic Sea
Black Sea
Aegean Sea
Adriatic Sea
Mediterranean Sea
Bay of Biscay

Carpathians
The Alps
Pyrenees
Corsica
Sardinia

Dnieper
Dniester
Danube
Vistula
Elbe
Rhine
Seine
Loire
Rhône
Po
Ebro
Tagus
Dvina

1352
1351
1350
1349
1348
1347

13

MEDIEVAL BRITAIN

On Christmas Day 1066 William of Normandy was crowned King of England after defeating the English King Harold in the Battle of Hastings. The following year he set about establishing control over his Anglo-Saxon subjects, ruthlessly suppressing any signs of revolt. The lands of the English nobility were distributed among the Norman barons, thus hastening the disappearance of the Anglo-Saxon way of life. In its place, Norman institutions and culture flourished, with Norman French becoming the language of the courts and society. Under a succession of Norman kings, England's prosperity grew and the number of towns rose rapidly. In the countryside a system of feudalism developed, under which each man received land, or the right to work land, in return for services provided to his lord. However, in the second half of the 14th century there were already signs – such as the Peasants' Revolt of 1381 – that the end of feudalism was fast approaching.

England in 1086
- Shire boundary
- Marcher (border) earldom
- Former marcher (border) earldom

SCOTLAND
NORTH-UMBERLAND
CUMBRIA
ST CUTHBERT'S LAND
YORKSHIRE
TWIXT RIBBLE AND MERSEY
CHESTER
DERBY
NOTTINGHAM
LINCOLN
TO NOTTS
HUNTINGDON
STAFFORD
LEICESTER
SHREWS-BURY
WALES
WARWICK
NORTHAMPTON
NORFOLK
CAM-BRIDGE
SUFFOLK
HEREFORD
WORCESTER
BED-FORD
BUCKINGHAM
HERTFORD
ESSEX
GLOUCESTER
OXFORD
MIDDLESEX
BERKSHIRE
WILTSHIRE
HAMPSHIRE
SURREY
KENT
SOMERSET
SUSSEX
DEVON
DORSET
CORNWALL

The Norman Conquest under William I 1066–87

- → Movements of Harold II in 1066
- → Movements of William of Normandy in 1066
- → Movements of William I 1067–81
- 🏰 Castle built 1066–87
- ✕ Battle
- ↓ Naval presence

SCOTLAND
1072
Newcastle-on-Tyne
Durham
1069
Stamford Bridge ✕ 25 Sept 1066
York
✕ 20 Sept 1066
Fulford
1070
1068 and 1069
Lincoln
Chester
Nottingham
Stafford
Shrewsbury
Rockingham
Hunting-don
Norwich
Warwick
Worcester
Hereford
Northampton
WALES
Ely
1071
St David's
1081
Cambridge
Gloucester
Colchester
Oxford
Dec 1066
Wallingford
Windsor
London
Rochester
Sandwich
Canterbury
Dover
1068
Salisbury
Winchester
Bramber Lewes
✕ 14 Oct 1066
Exeter
Arundel
Pevensey ↓ 28 Sept 1066
Hastings
FRANCE
Totnes

◀ In mid-September 1066 King Harold of England marched north to confront an army led by his brother Tostig and Harold Hardrada of Norway. He won a resounding victory at the Battle of Stamford Bridge but then had to march south to fight William of Normandy, who had landed at Pevensey on 28 September. By the time Harold's army reached the coast it was exhausted, thus helping to ensure a Norman victory in the Battle of Hastings on 14 October. After the battle William marched swiftly to London where he was crowned king. From 1067 he dealt swiftly with any signs of opposition from the English and built castles throughout the land to establish Norman control.

◄ In 1086, the year in which the Domesday Survey was completed, England consisted of a pattern of shires which was to last, with only minor changes, until 1974. On the Welsh and Scottish borders there were 'marcher earldoms' which William had created as a means of defending the frontier areas. For the Domesday Survey, information was collected in each shire about the chief towns, the lands of the king and lands of the tenants-in-chief. It showed that since 1066, 1500 foreigners had received lands from the king, and English landholders had almost disappeared.

The Peasants' Revolt 1381

➤ Route of Wat Tyler

☸ Main centre of rebellion

England, Wales and Scotland in 1400

⌂ Castle

⊗ Fair

○ Cinque port

— Border between English shires and Wales

— Border of Principality of Wales

▲ The Peasants' Revolt of 1381 was mainly a revolt of farmers and tradesmen, with a following of farm labourers, who were angry over the imposition of a very high poll tax. It began in a village in Essex when a tax-collector was killed, and spread quickly to other villages and towns in the southeast. However, the revolt only became a serious threat when a large band of men from Essex and Kent marched to London under the leadership of Wat Tyler. They secured a promise from the king that their demands would be met, but after Tyler was killed by the Mayor of London, the revolt collapsed.

◄ At the end of the 14th century there were stone castles in every part of the country, many built by the Norman kings as a means of establishing their authority. Some were in the middle of flourishing towns, where an enormous variety of crafts and trades were practised. Several towns were also the sites of great fairs. These were held each year and often attracted merchants from as far afield as Flanders, Spain and Germany. A growing volume of trade with these countries was handled by the ports on the south and east coasts.

KINGDOM OF SCOTLAND

Irish Sea

North Sea

PRINCIPALITY OF WALES

MARCH OF WALES

English Channel

STATES AND EMPIRES IN EUROPE c.1500–1750

In the 16th century none of the states or empires in mainland Europe were ruled by strong central governments. All were made up of territories that were controlled more by local princes or nobles than by a king or emperor. The ruling dynasties, such as the Habsburgs of Spain and Austria, frequently went to war to establish their claim to various lands. There was also constant warfare in the 17th century, but after 1660 there was a move towards centralisation, most notably in France under King Louis XIV.

▼ From the 15th century the empire established by the Ottoman Turks was one of the most militarily effective states of all time, and in the Christian world its sultan was regarded with great respect. Its decline began in 1683 when a Turkish army laying siege to Vienna was destroyed. However, in the 18th century it was still the largest empire in Europe and western Asia.

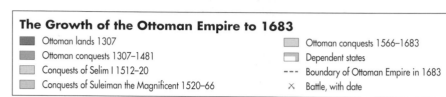

The Growth of the Ottoman Empire to 1683

- Ottoman lands 1307
- Ottoman conquests 1307–1481
- Conquests of Selim I 1512–20
- Conquests of Suleiman the Magnificent 1520–66
- Ottoman conquests 1566–1683
- Dependent states
- --- Boundary of Ottoman Empire in 1683
- ✕ Battle, with date

The Growth of the Russian Empire

- Russian territory 1462
- Acquisitions 1462–1533
- Acquisitions 1533–1598
- Acquisitions 1598–1619
- Acquisitions 1619–1689
- Occupied by Russia 1644–89
- Acquisitions 1689–1796
- ⌂ Trading post/fortress (ostrog), with date of foundation
- **SAM** Native people

▼ In the mid-15th century the Russian state of Muscovy was one of many small states in northern Europe that paid tribute to the Tatars. By the end of the 18th century it was at the heart of an immense land empire that stretched from the Baltic in the west, across Siberia, to the Bering Strait in the east.

▶ Frontiers changed considerably between 1500 and 1560. In 1500, for example, the Habsburgs were just one of a number of ancient dynasties. By the 1520s they had accumulated under Emperor Charles V the largest conglomeration of territories in Europe since the 9th century.

Kazan

Nizhniy Novgorod

RUSSIA

FINLAND

Moscow

SWEDEN

ESTONIA

LIVONIA

Riga

COURLAND

Stockholm

LITHUANIA

PRUSSIA

Baltic Sea

Warsaw

POLAND

VOLHYNIA

GALICIA

PODOLIA

UKRAINE

KHANATE OF CRIMEA

Sea of Azov

Black Sea

ANATOLIA

SYRIA

Cyprus

OTTOMAN EMPIRE

EGYPT

Mediterranean Sea

Rhodes

Constantinople

NORWAY

Oslo

DENMARK

Copenhagen

Danzig

SILESIA

BRANDENBURG

Berlin

Prague

BOHEMIA

ROYAL HUNGARY

Krakow

Vienna

Buda

Pest

TURKISH HUNGARY

Belgrade

SERBIA

BOSNIA

CROATIA

RAGUSA

MONTE-NEGRO

ALBANIA

BULGARIA

Sofia

Bucharest

WALLACHIA

MOLDAVIA

TRANSYLVANIA

MOREA

Athens

Crete

HOLY ROMAN EMPIRE

Hamburg

SAXONY

HESSE

Cologne

PALATINATE

WÜRTT.

EMBURG

BAVARIA

Munich

SWISS CONFEDERATION

Berne

Milan

Venice

Turin

SAVOY

LORRAINE

Genoa

Florence

Rome

PAPAL STATES

Naples

NAPLES

Palermo

Sicily

Tripoli
1510-51

Hamburg

Amsterdam

Brussels

NORMANDY

Paris

FRANCE

Lyons

BRITTANY

Corsica
(to Genoa)

Sardinia

TUNIS

Tunis
1535-75

Biserta
1535-74

Bugia
1510-55

Algiers
1510-29

ALGIERS

Balearic Is

North Sea

Shetland Is

Orkney Is

Edinburgh

SCOTLAND

ENGLAND

WALES

London

Dublin

IRELAND

Atlantic Ocean

ROUSSILLON

NAVARRE

ARAGON

SPAIN

Madrid

CASTILE

GRANADA

Oran
1509-1706

Melilla
1496

Tangier
1471-1580

PORTUGAL

Lisbon

Europe c.1560

—	Boundary of the Holy Roman Empire	
	Austrian Habsburg territories	
	Spanish Habsburg Territories	
	Ottoman Empire	
	Tributary to the Ottoman Empire	
	Venetian territories	
	Major German secular states	

NEW PERSPECTIVES IN 16TH-CENTURY EUROPE

In the second half of the 16th century, Europeans embarked on an era of exploration, during which they discovered a sea route around Africa to India and Southeast Asia, and the existence of the Americas. The first circum-navigation of the globe was achieved in 1519–21, and from this point Europeans began to think of the oceans of the world as one vast area of communication. At the same time, both Church and society were transformed by the Protestant Reformation. Beginning as a response to the Catholic Church's reputation for corruption, it resulted in the establishment of Protestant churches in many countries in Europe.

▼ Lutheran, Zwinglian and Calvinist churches were among those established as a result of the Protestant Reformation. In response, the Catholic Church undertook many internal reforms.

The Protestant and Catholic Reformations

- Area where reformed faith dominant by 1580
- Area where reformed faith growing c. 1560–70
- Area where considerable local reformed faith c. 1560–70
- Area where some penetration of reform c. 1560–70
- Area that remained predominantly Catholic
- Area where Lutheranism adopted, with date
- Area where Zwinglianism or Calvinism adopted, with date
- Area where other Protestant Church established (Anglican, Polish, Bohemian)
- † Catholic mission and reform endeavour, with date

Voyages of Exploration 1450–1600

- **1587** Date of Portuguese discovery in Africa
- **Davis** Name of explorer with date of voyage
- ↑ Explorers on behalf of Spain
- ↑ Explorers on behalf of Portugal
- ↑ Explorers on behalf of France
- ↑ Explorers on behalf of England
- ↑ Explorers on behalf of the Dutch
- ⋮ The world known of by Europeans c.1450

Routes Across the Pacific

- ↑ Explorers on behalf of Spain
- ↑ Explorers on behalf of England

▲ Portuguese explorers led the way in searching for a sea route to the Spice Islands in the east, travelling down the coast of West Africa between 1415 and 1460. In 1488 Dias reached the Cape of Good Hope and in 1497–98 da Gama reached India. Meanwhile, the Spaniards searched in a westerly direction. The result was that between 1492 and 1502 the West Indies and Venezuelan coast were discovered by Columbus. The Spaniards went on to pioneer the route across the Pacific while the British and French explored the coast of North America.

TUDOR BRITAIN

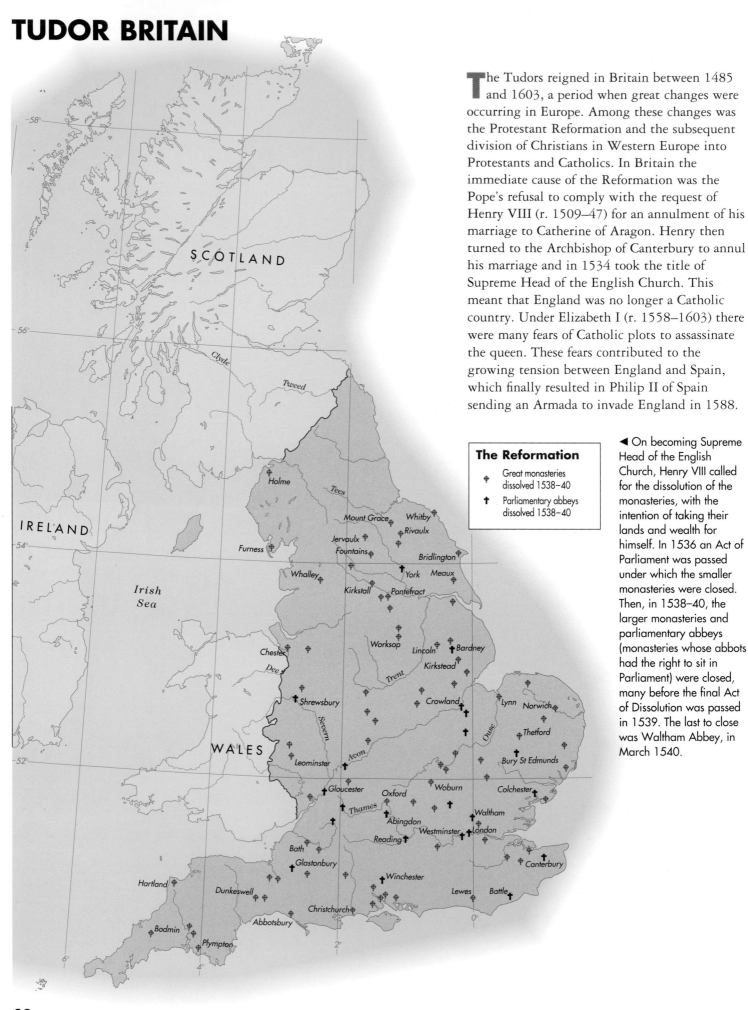

The Tudors reigned in Britain between 1485 and 1603, a period when great changes were occurring in Europe. Among these changes was the Protestant Reformation and the subsequent division of Christians in Western Europe into Protestants and Catholics. In Britain the immediate cause of the Reformation was the Pope's refusal to comply with the request of Henry VIII (r. 1509–47) for an annulment of his marriage to Catherine of Aragon. Henry then turned to the Archbishop of Canterbury to annul his marriage and in 1534 took the title of Supreme Head of the English Church. This meant that England was no longer a Catholic country. Under Elizabeth I (r. 1558–1603) there were many fears of Catholic plots to assassinate the queen. These fears contributed to the growing tension between England and Spain, which finally resulted in Philip II of Spain sending an Armada to invade England in 1588.

The Reformation

✤ Great monasteries dissolved 1538–40

✝ Parliamentary abbeys dissolved 1538–40

◄ On becoming Supreme Head of the English Church, Henry VIII called for the dissolution of the monasteries, with the intention of taking their lands and wealth for himself. In 1536 an Act of Parliament was passed under which the smaller monasteries were closed. Then, in 1538–40, the larger monasteries and parliamentary abbeys (monasteries whose abbots had the right to sit in Parliament) were closed, many before the final Act of Dissolution was passed in 1539. The last to close was Waltham Abbey, in March 1540.

The Spanish Armada in 1588

→ Main route of Armada
→ Route of English fleet
✕ Battle
⚓ Spanish shipwreck
⚡ Major storm

Atlantic Ocean

Shetland
20 August
Fair Isle
Orkney
Firth of Forth
Malin Head
Rossan Point
Erris Head
Killybegs
Fair Head
Clare Island
Sligo
Galway
Dublin
Dingle Bay
North Sea
London
Margate
8 August
Dover
Calais
6 August
Exeter
Portland Bill
Isle of Wight
Plymouth
The Lizard
31 July
2 August
3 August

Plymouth
Dover
26 July
18 September
Corunna
19 June
Santander
21 September
Lisbon
29 May

▲ The Spanish Armada, consisting of 130 ships, set sail from Lisbon in May 1588, but did not arrive in the English Channel until July. It had a number of minor battles with English ships before reaching Calais, where the intention was to pick up an army of 17,000 men. The English sent fireships into the port, and in the resulting chaos many Spanish ships were destroyed by their opponents' gunnery. The Spaniards then turned north and were pursued as far as the Firth of Forth. They subsequently ran into more storms, and when they finally returned home in September more than half their ships were missing.

N

Islington
Fleet Ditch
Tottenham Court
Bethnal Green
Marylebone
Spital Fields
Mile End
Mile End Road
Lincoln's Inn Fields
Smithfield
Bishopsgate
Leicester Fields
Covent Garden
Fleet Street
St Paul's Cathedral
Somerset House
Temple
St James's Palace
Strand
Savoy
The Clink
Whitehall Palace
Lambeth Marsh
Globe Theatre
London Bridge
Tower
Westminster
Westminster Palace
Southwark
Rotherhithe
River Thames
Westminster Abbey
Lambeth Palace
Bermondsey
Horse Ferry
Lambeth

0   1 mile
0   1.5 km

Late Tudor London
■ Built-up area

◄ The population of London grew from about 120,000 in 1550 to almost 200,000 in 1600. Most of these extra people lived in wooden and unsanitary housing that was built to the east of the Tower of London, in suburbs such as Whitechapel and Stepney. To the west, in an almost continuous line that ran along the north side of the Thames for over a mile, there were many splendid palaces surrounded by large gardens. On the south side of the river there were far fewer buildings, but it was here that the first theatre was opened in 1577. The Globe Theatre, at which Shakespeare's plays were performed, was opened in 1599.

BRITAIN 1600–1750

In 1603 King James VI of Scotland became King James I of England, although the two kingdoms were not to be united until 1707. Thus began the reign of the Stuart dynasty uder which James's son, Charles I, was to become extremely unpopular. In 1640 Charles was forced to agree to a set of reforms that gave Parliament more power. These, however, were not considered by some people to be enough and in 1641 Parliament split into two groups – the Royalists (Cavaliers), who supported the King, and the Parliamentarians (Roundheads). The civil war that broke out between the two parties in 1642 was won by the Roundheads in 1646. A second civil war in 1648 led to the execution of Charles I in 1649 and the rise to political power of Oliver Cromwell. A skilled military leader, he was also ruthless in his determination to suppress any opposition, as his campaign in Ireland in 1649–53 demonstrated. His death was followed in 1660 by the restoration of the monarchy and the reigns of King Charles II and King James II.

Ireland in the 16th and 17th Centuries

- ☐ Boundary of the Pale c. 1550
- ◼ Areas in which English and Scots settled before 1653
- ☐ Land reserved for Irish 1653
- ✕ Battle or massacre with date

Scotland in the 18th Century

- —— Shire border
- ← Route of the Young Pretender 1745–46
- ✕ Battle with date

▲ English authority in Ireland was largely confined to a small area around Dublin, known as the Pale, until the late 15th century, when Henry VII began the settlement of the country by Englishmen. In 1653 Cromwell granted a comparatively small area of the country to Irish proprietors who had been loyal to Parliament.

▶ Throughout the English Civil War of 1642–46, the Parliamentarians kept control of London and the southeast while the Royalists were strongest in the north and west. The King used Oxford as his capital.

◀ In 1745 Prince Charles landed in Scotland with the aim of raising support for his campaign to win back the throne of England and Scotland for the Stuarts. His father, King James II, had been deposed in1688. Charles's campaign ended in disaster when his army of Scottish highlanders was defeated at the Battle of Culloden in April 1746.

The Civil War 1644-46

- Districts under control of Parliament at beginning of 1645
- Districts under control of King at end of 1645
- Districts conquered by Parliament during 1645
- ✕ Battle with date

North Sea

SCOTLAND

Irish Sea

English Channel

Newcastle
Carlisle
Scarborough
Bolton Castle
Hull
York
Marston Moor 1644 ✕
Sheffield
Newark
Belvoir Castle
Naseby 1645 ✕
Cropredy Bridge 1644 ✕
Norwich
Huntingdon
Cambridge
Colchester
Maidstone
Dover
London
Oxford
Basing House 1645 ✕
Winchester
Portsmouth
Newbury 1644 ✕
Southampton
Corfe Castle ✕
Liverpool
Rowton 1645 ✕
Nantwich 1644 ✕
Beeston Castle
Shrewsbury
Gloucester
Hereford
Langport 1645 ✕
Taunton
Exeter
Caernarfon
Pembroke
Lostwithiel 1644 ✕
Plymouth

The Civil War 1642-43

- Districts under control of King throughout 1643
- Districts under control of Parliament throughout 1643
- Districts conquered by King during 1643
- Districts conquered by Parliament during 1643
- ✕ Battle with date

North Sea

SCOTLAND

Irish Sea

English Channel

Newcastle
Carlisle
Scarborough
Bolton Castle
York
Hull 1643 ✕
Winceby 1643 ✕
Sheffield
Belvoir Castle
Norwich
Cambridge
Colchester
Maidstone
Dover
Leicester
Northampton
Brentford 1643 ✕
London
Arundel
Edge Hill 1642 ✕
Oxford
Newbury 1643 ✕
Portsmouth
Lichfield 1643 ✕
Roundway Down 1643 ✕
Southampton
Corfe Castle 1643 ✕
Preston 1643 ✕
Manchester
Liverpool
Chester
Lansdown Hill 1643 ✕
Bristol
Wardour Castle
Hereford
Raglan Castle
Exeter
Bideford 1643 ✕
Stratton 1643 ✕
Bradock Down 1643 ✕
Dartmouth 1643 ✕
Caernarfon
Pembroke

NORTH AMERICA 1500–1770

When Europeans arrived on the shores of North America in the 16th century, many different ways of life existed among the native inhabitants. Farming communities were established in large areas of the south, and in the southeast there were towns of up to 30,000 inhabitants. Elsewhere, people's livelihood depended to a varying extent on hunting, fishing, gathering, agriculture and trade. The Europeans attempted to found colonies, but none survived until the following century, when Britain, France, Spain and Holland created major empires on the mainland and in the Caribbean. Some Native Americans responded to the arrival of the Europeans by moving west. In the northeast a number of previously warring groups settled their differences and became involved in the wars between the rival European powers.

► Some Native American peoples had a nomadic way of life before the arrival of the Europeans. After the introduction of the horse by the Spaniards in the 16th century, they were able to travel great distances more easily.

▼ The horse revolutionised hunting techniques, enabling the regular and efficient slaughter of animals. In the 16th and 17th centuries many Plains tribes abandoned their traditional way of life, and adopted one based on horseback hunting, mainly of buffalo.

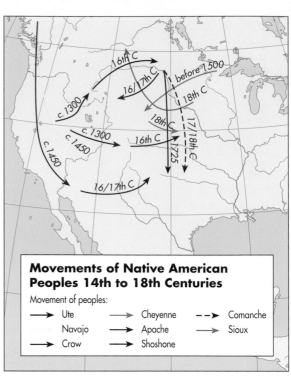

Movements of Native American Peoples 14th to 18th Centuries

Movement of peoples:

→ Ute	→ Cheyenne	- -▶ Comanche
→ Navajo	→ Apache	→ Sioux
→ Crow	→ Shoshone	

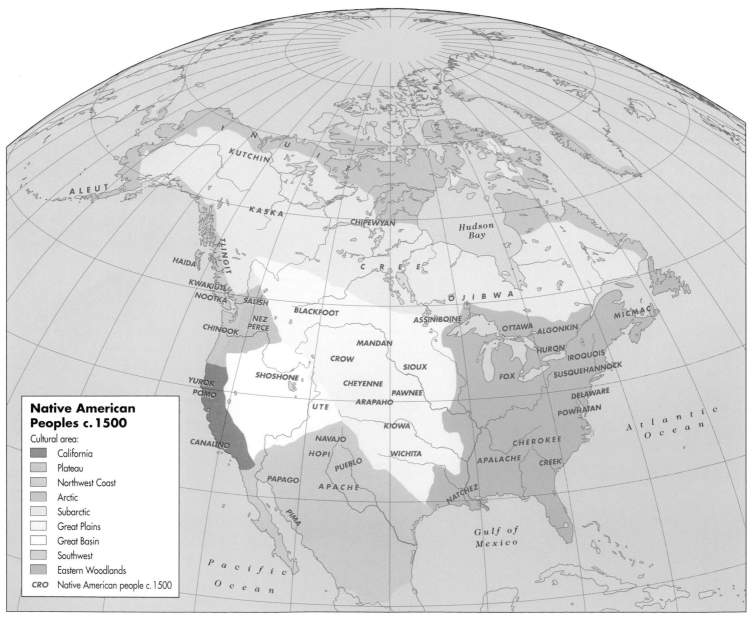

Native American Peoples c.1500

Cultural area:

- California
- Plateau
- Northwest Coast
- Arctic
- Subarctic
- Great Plains
- Great Basin
- Southwest
- Eastern Woodlands
- CRO Native American people c.1500

Colonisation of the North American Mainland to 1750

HUR Native American people

British settlement:
- to 1640
- to 1750
- frontier lands in 1750

Spanish settlement:
- to 1750
- frontier lands in 1750

French settlement:
- to 1750
- frontier lands in 1750

Economic activity c.1750:
- mixed agriculture
- fishing
- trapping
- cattle
- grain
- tobacco
- rice
- indigo
- timber
- shipbuilding
- ironworks
- trade route

Map labels: Hudson Bay, RUPERT'S LAND, NEWFOUNDLAND, St John's, St Lawrence, NOVA SCOTIA, MICMAC, Quebec, Three Rivers, Montreal, ALGONKIN, HURON, L Superior, L Huron, L Michigan, L Ontario, L Erie, FIVE NATIONS, Salem, Boston, RHODE ISLAND, Dutch 1616-64, New York, Philadelphia, Baltimore, Missouri, LOUISIANA, Arkansas, Jamestown, Norfolk, CHEROKEE, Savannah, Charleston, APALACHE, Santa Fé, Red River, El Paso, Rio Grande, Mississippi, San Antonio, New Orleans, Gulf of Mexico, The Bahamas, Tropic of Cancer, Atlantic Ocean

Trade route labels: timber, naval stores, furs, whale products; manufactures, mercantile services; tobacco, rice, indigo, naval stores, furs; slaves; rum, molasses; fish, timber, grain, rice, shipping services

▲ The British colonies on the mainland were set up in two main waves: from 1603 to 1634, when settlements were established in Virginia, Maryland and New England, and from 1664 to 1680, when the Carolinas and Pennsylvania were founded and New York was seized from the Dutch. In the early 17th century the French established fishing and trading colonies in Canada. Later, they colonised the area around the Mississippi, but by 1763 this was lost to the British and Spaniards.

▶ The British and French colonies in the Caribbean had an environment in which disease flourished. Consequently, in the early years the majority of immigrants to these colonies were white bondsmen, who provided several years of unpaid labour – usually on tobacco plantations – in exchange for the cost of their passage and a plot of free land. Around 1640 a shift from tobacco to sugar production increased the demand for labour and slaves began to be imported from Africa.

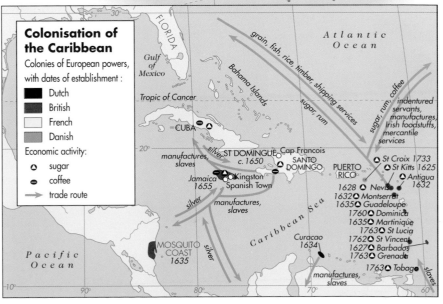

Colonisation of the Caribbean

Colonies of European powers, with dates of establishment:
- Dutch
- British
- French
- Danish

Economic activity:
- sugar
- coffee
- trade route

Atlantic Ocean, FLORIDA, Gulf of Mexico, Tropic of Cancer, Bahama Islands, CUBA, ST DOMINGUE c.1650, Cap Francois, SANTO DOMINGO, PUERTO RICO, St Croix 1733, St Kitts 1625, Antigua 1632, 1628 Nevis, 1632 Montserrat, 1635 Guadeloupe, 1760 Dominica, 1635 Martinique, 1763 St Lucia, 1762 St Vincent, 1627 Barbados, 1763 Grenada, 1763 Tobago, Jamaica 1655, Kingston, Spanish Town, Curacao 1634, MOSQUITO COAST 1635, Caribbean Sea, Pacific Ocean

*Trade route labels:* grain, fish, rice, timber shipping services; sugar, rum; sugar, rum, coffee; indentured servants, manufactures, Irish foodstuffs, mercantile services; silver; manufactures, slaves; slaves

ASIA 1500–1920

In the 16th century the Mughal Empire in India and the Ming Empire in China were two of the greatest powers in the world. By the end of the 18th century the Mughal Empire had only symbolic significance, and real power was in the hands of numerous princes and of the British. In China the Ming Dynasty had been replaced by the Manchus, and there was a growing threat from European powers who were eager to trade freely throughout Asia. When, in 1842, Britain forced the Manchus to lift the ban on the opium trade and open ports to European merchants, it was clear that China was no longer a world power.

Ming and Manchu Qing Imperial Borders

▓ Area under Ming Dynasty 1600	Rebuilding of the Great Wall in:
▒ Additional area under Manchu Dynasty in 1840	—— 14th century
▒ Additional area under Manchu Dynasty in 1840	– – – 15th–16th centuries
☐ Manchu vassal state	······ 16th century

► The Mughal Empire was founded in 1526 by Babur, the Sultan of Kabul. Under Babur's grandson Akbar (1556–1605), the empire was expanded and centralised. Domestic industries, trade, art and architecture all flourished. Aurangzeb (1658–1707) attempted to expand the empire southwards, but he was unable to deal effectively with his many opponents and the empire went into fast decline.

Mughal India

☐	Approximate extent of Mughal Empire 1605
▓	Additional area claimed by Mughals 1707
—	Boundaries of provinces (subahs) 1707
●	Provincial (subah) headquarters 1707
➤	Advance of Marathas
MA	People in rebellion against the empire c.1700

Major European trading posts by 1700:
☒ Portuguese	☒ British
☒ Danish	☒ French
☒ Dutch	

▲ Under the Ming Dynasty of 1368–1644, China's cultural, political and economic strength grew. The European powers presented no real threat, the Chinese navy twice succeeding in defeating Dutch fleets off the south coast in 1622–24. A more serious threat was posed by the nomadic Manchus who lived to the north of the Great Wall. In 1644 they seized control in Beijing and established a dynasty under which the Chinese Empire expanded to its greatest extent ever, encompassing Manchuria, Mongolia, Turkestan and Tibet. From 1800 onwards, the Manchus were increasingly under threat from uprisings caused by famine and a corrupt and inadequately funded government. Aggressive Western powers also played a part in undermining Manchu power, which finally came to an end in 1911 with a revolution that established China as a republic.

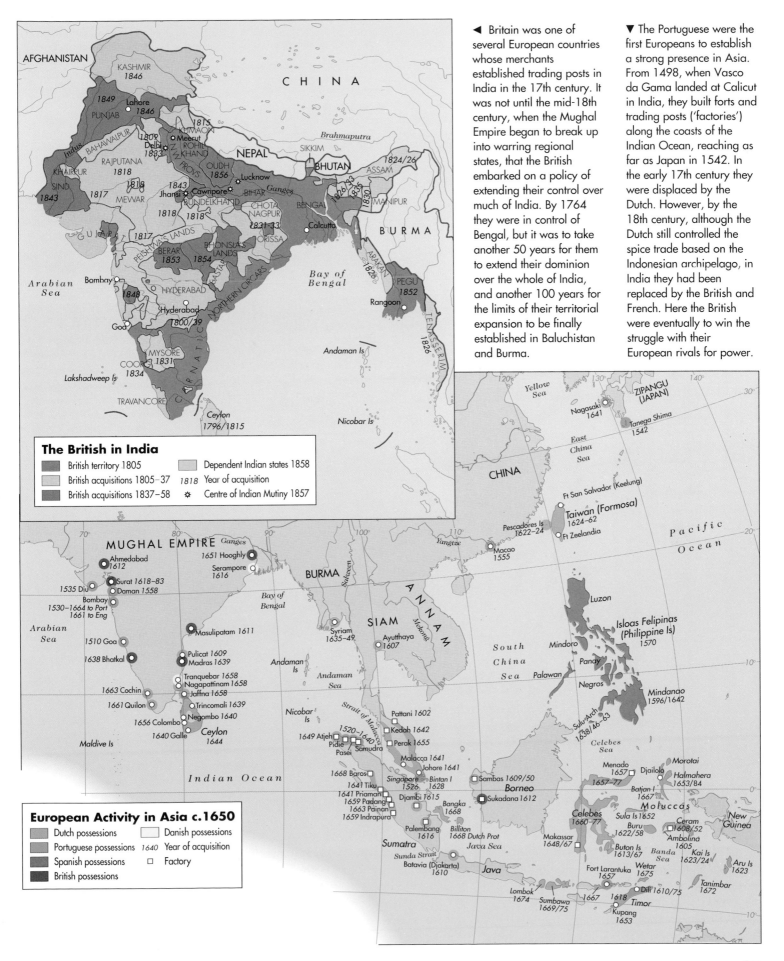

◀ Britain was one of several European countries whose merchants established trading posts in India in the 17th century. It was not until the mid-18th century, when the Mughal Empire began to break up into warring regional states, that the British embarked on a policy of extending their control over much of India. By 1764 they were in control of Bengal, but it was to take another 50 years for them to extend their dominion over the whole of India, and another 100 years for the limits of their territorial expansion to be finally established in Baluchistan and Burma.

▼ The Portuguese were the first Europeans to establish a strong presence in Asia. From 1498, when Vasco da Gama landed at Calicut in India, they built forts and trading posts ('factories') along the coasts of the Indian Ocean, reaching as far as Japan in 1542. In the early 17th century they were displaced by the Dutch. However, by the 18th century, although the Dutch still controlled the spice trade based on the Indonesian archipelago, in India they had been replaced by the British and French. Here the British were eventually to win the struggle with their European rivals for power.

The British in India

- British territory 1805
- British acquisitions 1805–37
- British acquisitions 1837–58
- Dependent Indian states 1858
- *1818* Year of acquisition
- ✿ Centre of Indian Mutiny 1857

European Activity in Asia c.1650

- Dutch possessions
- Portuguese possessions
- Spanish possessions
- British possessions
- Danish possessions
- *1640* Year of acquisition
- □ Factory

REVOLUTIONARY AND NAPOLEONIC EUROPE

Revolutionary France 1789–94

- Area of agrarian revolt early 1789
- Spread of the 'Great Fear' July–August 1789
- ○ Town ruled by revolutionary committee
- Major counter-revolutionary stronghold 1793
- Area of sustained counter-revolutionary resistance 1793
- Foreign territory fought over by France 1792–94
- Attack by foreign powers
- 4.93 Date of attack
- ⊗ French victory

British and Dutch

Hanoverians, Austrians 9.93

Brussels 7.93

Lille

Fleurus 6.94 9.93

Prussians 9.93

AUSTRIAN NETHERLANDS

English Channel

British 3.93

Amiens

Rouen

Reims

Metz

Valmy 9.92

Nancy

Strasbourg

Caen

NORMANDY

Seine

Paris

Troyes

ALSACE

Brest

BRITTANY

Rennes

Angers

Loire

Tours

Sancerre

Dijon

Besançon

Quiberon

3.93 Royalist émigrés

Nantes

Poitiers

Bourges

British 3.93

Limoges

Massif Central

Lyon

SAVOY

Grenoble

The Alps

Austrians 8.93

Sardinians 9.93

Bay of Biscay

Bordeaux

GIRONDE

Dordogne

Rhône

Montauban

Garonne

Toulouse

Nîmes

AVIGNON

Montpellier

Marseilles

Toulon

Mediterranean Sea

Spanish 4.93

Pyrenees

British and Spanish

◀ Early in 1789, following a poor harvest, peasants and industrial labourers in parts of France rioted. In Paris, meanwhile, the king had been forced to call a meeting of the Estates-General (parliament) in order to raise extra taxes. The representatives of the middle-classes (the 'Third Estate') took this opportunity to reject co-operation with the other two Estates (aristocracy and clergy) and declare themselves a National Assembly. Riots in Paris on 14 July 1789 spread throughout France, stirred up by revolutionary committees. Peasants looted and destroyed the property of the aristocracy in what became known as the 'Great Fear'. Foreign monarchs sent armies in an attempt to aid the French king, but this only hastened his execution, which took place in January 1793. During 1793 and 1794 France successfully defended itself against foreign invaders on all sides, and counter-revolutionary uprisings in the west and south.

The French Revolution began in July 1789 when the middle classes seized power at the same time as peasants and industrial workers were driven by poverty and starvation to riot against the property-owning aristocracy. Anti-monarchist feeling led to the execution of King Louis XIV in January 1793. A reign of terror ensued, during which 40,000 people were executed, when extremists, led by Robespierre, sought to impose the revolution. From mid-1794 a more moderate faction gained power, but this was overthrown in 1799 by Napoleon, who became First Consul of France. He oversaw major reforms of French government, including the drafting of the Napoleonic Civil Code, which became the basis of legal systems in many countries. In 1804 he proclaimed himself Emperor – an act many considered a betrayal of revolutionary principles.

Vitoria 6.1813

Corunna 1.1809

Valladolid 7.1808

Sarag 2.1

Salamanca 7.1812

Somosierra 11.180

Madrid

PORTUGAL

Talavera 7.1809

SPAIN

Vimeiro 8.1808

Trafalgar 10.1805

European Coalitions 1793–1815

—— First Coalition 1793–96 —— Fourth Coalition 1806–7
—— Second Coalition 1798–99 —— Fifth Coalition 1809–15
—— Third Coalition 1805

◀ The French Revolution caused concern among the rulers of other European countries. Initially they feared a spread of revolutionary fervour to their own countries; later it became clear that the main threat was of invasion, as Napoleon attempted, by the use of military power, to impose his legal and administrative systems across Europe. Opposition to Napoleon's France brought together the European powers in a succession of coalitions. Britain was a constant member, with other countries joining when it was in their interest to do so. Russia also joined all five coalitions but, following its defeat in 1807, became an ally of France until 1810.

▼ Napoleon rose to fame as a general, with success in Italy in the 1790s. Despite a failed attempt to cut British trade routes in Egypt, he swept to power in 1799. He then embarked on a process of extending French rule across Europe. Spain became a French puppet state until the Spaniards revolted in 1808 and, supported by the Fifth Coalition, fought the Peninsular War. Napoleon's invasion of Russia in 1812 failed, however, when French supply lines were stretched and his troops were forced to retreat. Napoleon was captured in France in 1814, escaped, and was defeated at Waterloo on 18 June 1815.

Napoleonic Europe 1796–1815

- France 1792
Area under direct French rule during period 1792–1815:
- for more than 10 years
- 5–10 years
- less than 5 years
- Satellite regimes in 1810
—— Area within which departmental administration introduced
⊗ French victory
⊗ French defeat

Wars against:
- First Coalition 1796–97
- Third Coalition 1805
- Fifth Coalition 1809–15 (including Peninsular War 1808–14, Austrian War 1809, Russian Campaign 1812–13, War of Liberation 1813, Campaign of 1814–15) Egyptian Campaign 1788–89
- Second Coalition 1798–99
- Fourth Coalition 1806–7

INDEPENDENCE IN NORTH AMERICA

The American Revolution 1775–83

- ⊗ British victory
- ⊗ American victory
- ✕ No decisive victory
- ➡ British troop or naval movements
- ➡ American troop or naval movements
- ↓ French naval presence
- — Proclamation line of 1763

The American War of Independence, or American Revolution, broke out in 1775 as a response to resentment felt by the American colonists against their British rulers, and in particular to a series of taxes imposed on imported goods. The American Congress denounced the new taxes, and when the British government refused to back down, war broke out. The British were defeated in 1781, after the French, Spanish and Dutch had all joined forces with the Americans. A new constitution became law in 1788 and the 13 ex-colonies, each with its own government, formed the United States of America. Over the next 100 years American settlers moved further and further west, seeking farming land or gold to mine. The Indian Removal Act of 1830 resulted in the forced migration of all Native Americans from east of the Mississippi into what was designated 'Indian Territory'. During the 19th century, however, settlers encroached on this land; a series of bloody conflicts resulted as attempts were made to confine the Native Americans to reservations.

◀ After failing to capture Quebec at the end of 1775, the Americans began to secure victories in 1777. The war effectively ended in October 1781 when the British were defeated by the French navy and the American army at Yorktown.

Territorial Expansion from 1783

- The United States 1783
- Louisiana Purchase 1803
- West Florida annexation 1810, 1813
- East Florida ceded by Spain 1819
- Acquired from Britain 1818, 1842
- Texas annexation 1845
- Oregon County 1846
- Ceded by Mexico 1848
- Gadsden Purchase 1853
- *1837* Date of admission as state

▶ In the Treaty of Paris in 1783 the British gave up all claim to the 13 colonies and granted the Americans rights over all territory south of Canada and north of Mexico, as far west as the Mississippi. Between 1803 and 1853 the newly formed United States expanded westwards to the Pacific by a series of financial deals, negotiated settlements and forcible annexations. As each new territory was colonised by American settlers, and a viable government formed, it was eligible to join the United States of America.

Routes of Exploration and Settlement

Routes of:
—— Lewis and Clark 1804–6
—— Pike 1804–7
—— Long 1817–23
—— Settlers' trail
- - - Cattle trail
◎ Mining, with date when it began

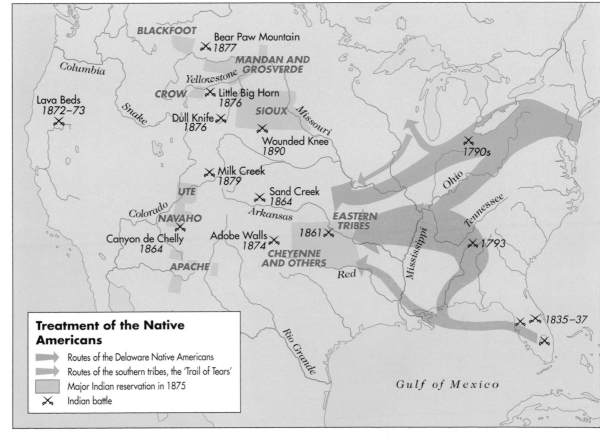

Treatment of the Native Americans

▷ Routes of the Delaware Native Americans
▷ Routes of the southern tribes, the 'Trail of Tears'
▨ Major Indian reservation in 1875
✗ Indian battle

▲ By 1800 the region east of the Mississippi was well explored, as was the west coast of America. By 1806 a government-funded expedition, led by Lewis and Clark, had established a route between the two. Alternative overland routes were established by settlers seeking land or gold. Other routes were used by farmers bringing cattle to the slaughterhouses.

▶ During the 18th century the Native Americans from Delaware made a slow westward migration and in 1830 the Indian Removal Act forced the southern tribes to move west too. Demands by white settlers for more land led to the Indian reservations and a series of bloody conflicts, as the Native Americans resisted attempts to restrict them to the reservations.

AFRICA AND THE SLAVE TRADE

▼ At the beginning of the 19th century there were few Europeans in Africa outside the coastal regions of the north, west and south. The internal trading network was controlled by independent kingdoms which, as the century progressed, came under threat both from Europeans and from the southward advance of Islam.

After exploring the west coast of Africa between 1420 and 1460, the Portuguese began to trade in slaves, acquiring them in exchange for firearms and manufactured goods, and shipping them across the Atlantic to the Americas. Other European nations quickly became involved in the trade, and between 1450 and 1900 over 12 million slaves were sent to work on plantations producing a variety of crops in North and South America and the Caribbean. However, at the beginning of the 19th century the interior of Africa, with its many independent kingdoms, was still little known to outsiders. It would be another 80 years before the European powers would begin to divide up the continent amongst themselves.

Principal African and European Trading Routes c.1840

Areas controlled by non-African powers:

- Britain
- France
- Oman
- Portugal
- Spain
- Ottoman Empire

TEKE African state or ethnic group

— African trade route

← Slave route

Slave Economies of the Western Hemisphere

— International boundary c.1830

Economic activity in which slaves employed:

- cotton
- rice and indigo
- tobacco
- coffee
- sugar
- mining
- mixed agriculture

○ Slave population (in thousands) c.1800
○ Slave population (in thousands) c.1860

1852 Date of emancipation

UNITED STATES OF AMERICA
1865

Southern United States
c. 1860
3724

Southern United States
c. 1800
848

Baltimore

Norfolk

Charleston
Savannah

Pensacola

St Augustine

New Orleans

French
Louisiana
11

Atlantic
Ocean

Bahamas

Spanish
West Indies

Mississippi

20
Mexico and
Spanish Central America

Rio Grande

MEXICO
1829

Gulf of
Mexico

CUBA
1886

170.5

Danish
Antilles *1848*

SANTO DOMINGO
1822

20

Leeward Islands

Mexico City

Vera Cruz

ST DOMINGUE
1794

PUERTO
RICO
1873

Guadeloupe

French
West Indies
643.4

Belize City

Jamaica

1834

British
West Indies
523.9

Windward
Islands

Martinique
1848

Barbados

P a c i f i c

UNITED PROVINCES
OF CENTRAL AMERICA
1824

Caribbean Sea

Guatemala
City

PANAMA
1824

Cartagena

Caracas

VENEZUELA
1854

BRITISH
GUIANA

DUTCH
GUIANA
1863

FRENCH
GUIANA

100

12

Equator

90

Bogotá

COLOMBIA
1852

O c e a n

Amazon

NORTHERN
BRAZIL

Northern
Brazil
347

Recife

Ecuador and
Colombia

50

ECUADOR
1854

EMPIRE OF
BRAZIL
1888

San Francisco

Salvador

Interior
Brazil
238

INTERIOR
BRAZIL

PERU
1854

BOLIVIA

Southern
Brazil
142

Rio de Janeiro

SOUTHERN
BRAZIL

PARAGUAY
1869

Paraná

30

ARGENTINA
1853

Buenos Aires

URUGUAY
1853

CHILE
1825

10

PATAGONIA

▼ Slaves were transported across the Atlantic in such appalling conditions that many died long before they reached the Americas. The British made the trade illegal in 1807, and the Americans in 1810, but other countries defied these bans for many years afterwards. More than three million slaves were sent across the Atlantic in the 19th century alone.

Arctic Circle

NORTH
AMERICA

EUROPE

North
Atlantic
Ocean

AFRICA

Equator

Pacific
Ocean

SOUTH
AMERICA

South
Atlantic
Ocean

Southern
Ocean

Transatlantic Slave Trade

→ Slave trade route

◄ In all the European empires in the Americas, the majority of slaves were employed on plantations, where they were underfed, overworked and ravaged by disease. The abolition of slavery was a long process which took place between the 1820s and 1880s and began in South America.

THE INDUSTRIAL REVOLUTION IN BRITAIN

Until the 1750s in Britain, cloth and other goods were manufactured in small, home-based industries. In the second half of the 18th century the invention of machines for spinning thread and for weaving material, and the development of steam engines that could drive this machinery, led to the building of large factories, often employing hundreds of workers. The goods produced by the factories were initially transported by water, but from 1825 onwards a railway network was developed. Britain's population almost trebled from 1750 to 1850, with more than half the people living in towns or cities by the end of the period.

The Cotton Textile Industry 1850

Irish Sea

to Preston
to Humber
1843
1841 to Leeds
Bury
Bolton
Rochdale
Wigan
1830
Manchester/ Salford
to Sheffield 1841
375 22
Liverpool
400 22
Mersey
Duke of Bridgewater 1761–77
to Birmingham 1842
Trent and Mersey 1777
Grand Junction 1837
Macclesfield

Legend		
—— Navigable river	Coalfield	Population of city in '000s for 1750 (inner) and 1850 (outer)
┴┴┴ Canal	# Cotton factories	
—— Railway		

Resources and Development in England 1750

Coalfield

—— Navigable river

Industries:

#	fustian and linen cloth
✿	woollen cloth
◪	copper mining and smelting
◪	tin mining and smelting
⊡	iron extraction and smelting
⚙	metalware and cutlery
⛴	shipbuilding

Carlisle

Ouse
Derwent

Preston
Bradford
Leeds
Barnsley
Manchester
Liverpool
Sheffield
Mersey
Lincoln
Trent
Nottingham

Irish Sea

Ironbridge
Birmingham
Welland
Nene
Norwich
Severn
Worcester
Avon
Northampton
Gt Ouse
Cambridge
Ipswich
Wye

Gloucester
Oxford
Swansea
Cardiff
Thames
London
Bristol
Bath
Dover

Exe
Southampton
Portsmouth
Brighton
Avon

Exeter
Dorchester
English Channel
50°

Falmouth
Plymouth

5°
0°

▲ While early factories were powered by waterwheels, and therefore had to be sited next to running water, the development of steam power from the 1780s onwards meant that factories were increasingly sited where they could easily be supplied with coal and raw materials. Large urban centres sprang up, linked by canals and railways. Lancashire, close to coalfields and with a well-established textile industry, became a major industrial region, with a rapidly developing transport network. By the 1830s one-third of its population was employed in the cotton factories and related industries.

◄ In 1750 most people lived in the countryside. Some worked on the land, but many produced cloth and smelted metals in small, home-based industries. London was the largest manufacturing centre, producing silk, gin, soap and glass.

Industry in Britain 1850

Industries:

#	cotton cloth
○	woollen cloth
✳	hosiery
♠	pottery
▲	copper mining and smelting
◻	tin mining and smelting
▣	iron extraction and smelting
◈	lead mining
✿	metalware and cutlery
△	salt, soap, chemicals and glass manufacture
⊥⊥⊥	shipbuilding
⬡	engineering

▢ Coalfield	······ Major canal
■ Major port	— Major railway
— Navigable river	

◀ By 1850 Britain's textile production had outstripped that of any other country. (Between 1750 and 1830 it had increased twelvefold.) The need for coal to power the factories had led to further development of the coalfields and to the building of an extensive canal system to transport coal to the factories, and finished goods to customers and to the ports. The human cost was, however, tremendous. The crowded and insanitary living conditions of the urban factory workers, as well as the long hours they were forced to work in dangerous factories, resulted in death rates considerably higher than those in rural areas. It was accepted that children as young as six years of age would work up to 14 hours a day in factories and in the mines.

Dundee

Glasgow Edinburgh

Newcastle
Sunderland

North Sea

Irish Sea

Bradford Leeds Hull
Rochdale Preston
Bury Halifax
Bolton
St Helens
Liverpool Manchester Sheffield

Holyhead

Stoke on Trent Nottingham
Derby
Leicester

Birmingham Norwich
Coventry
Cambridge

Swansea Harwich
Cardiff
Bristol London
Bath Chatham Canterbury
Dover
Exeter Southampton
Portsmouth

Plymouth

Falmouth

English Channel

INDUSTRIALISATION AND IMPERIALISM

The Industrial Revolution, which began in Britain in the late 18th century, had spread to northwest Europe and to the eastern United States by the mid-19th century. Many of the industrialising countries benefited from the experience of British engineers, who were employed in the building of factories and in the development of the railway system. By 1900

Britain, which had been unrivalled in 1850, had been overtaken by the USA as the world's leading manufacturing nation. For many countries, industrialisation went hand in hand with imperialism. They competed to secure domination over Asia, Africa and other parts of the world, seeking new sources of raw materials and markets for their manufactured products.

▼ Industrialisation in 19th-century Europe (as is clear from the development of the rail network) started in northern France, Belgium, the Netherlands and northern Germany, and spread to Spain, Italy and Austria-Hungary as the century progressed.

Industrialisation in Europe in the 19th Century

— International boundary 1871

Major railway lines constructed:
— by 1848
— 1848–1870
--- 1870–1914

Industry c. 1870:
- coal mining
- iron working
- textile production

Industry c. 1914:
- ⊡ steel
- ○ engineering
- ⚓ shipbuilding
- ◇ chemicals
- ⚡ electrical industry

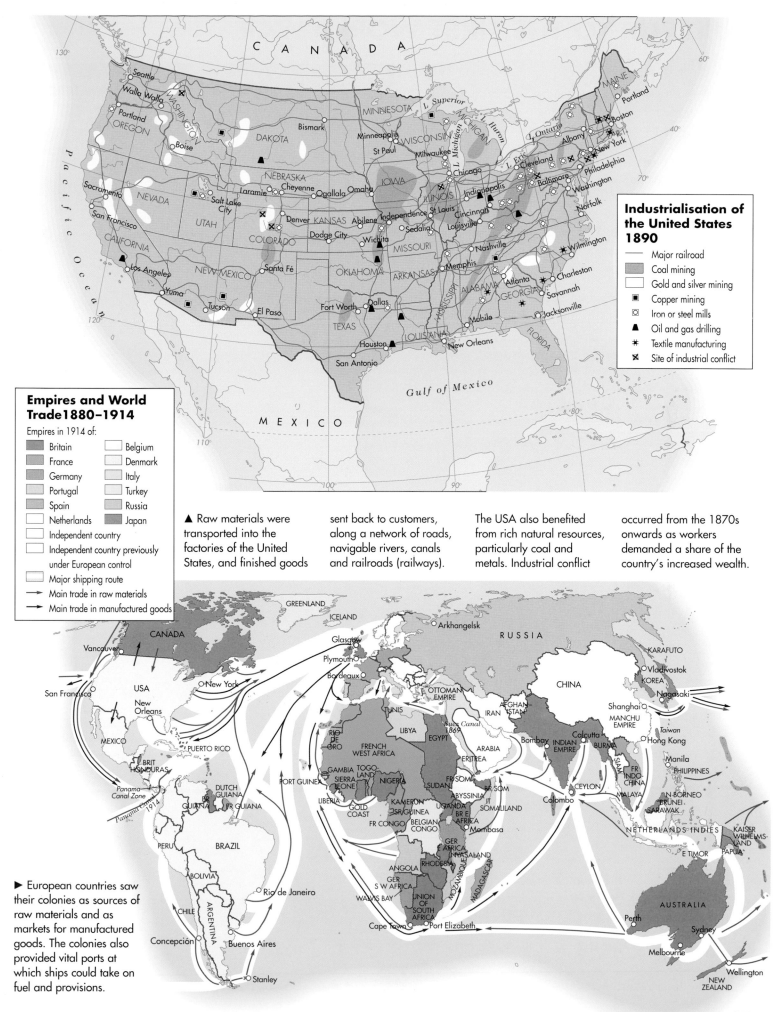

Industrialisation of the United States 1890

— Major railroad
▨ Coal mining
☐ Gold and silver mining
■ Copper mining
◉ Iron or steel mills
▲ Oil and gas drilling
✳ Textile manufacturing
✖ Site of industrial conflict

Empires and World Trade 1880–1914

Empires in 1914 of:

Britain
France
Germany
Portugal
Spain
Netherlands
Independent country
Independent country previously under European control
Major shipping route
→ Main trade in raw materials
→ Main trade in manufactured goods

Belgium
Denmark
Italy
Turkey
Russia
Japan

▲ Raw materials were transported into the factories of the United States, and finished goods sent back to customers, along a network of roads, navigable rivers, canals and railroads (railways). The USA also benefited from rich natural resources, particularly coal and metals. Industrial conflict occurred from the 1870s onwards as workers demanded a share of the country's increased wealth.

▶ European countries saw their colonies as sources of raw materials and as markets for manufactured goods. The colonies also provided vital ports at which ships could take on fuel and provisions.

BUILD-UP TO THE FIRST WORLD WAR

The outbreak of war in 1914 was the result of a number of factors. The creation by 1871 of a militarily powerful and rapidly industrialising Germany was seen as threatening by France, Russia and the United Kingdom. Germany's alliances with Austria-Hungary in the early 1880s supported this view and prompted France, which had lost Alsace-Lorraine following defeat by Germany in the war of 1870–71, to ally itself with Russia in 1893. The UK, which had pursued an isolationist policy since the early years of the 19th century, briefly considered allying with Germany, but became alarmed by that country's huge military investment, and decided to side with France and Russia. This system of alliances might have resulted in a peaceful balance of power but for competition between Austria and Russia for control of the Balkans that led ultimately to the outbreak of war across Europe and the Middle East.

European Alliances 1882
▨ Country in Three Emperors' Alliance 1881
▱ Country in Triple Alliance 1882

The Balkans 1878–1914

- – – Border of country or province 1878
- —— Border of country 1914
- ▱ Austro-Hungarian Empire 1878
- ▨ Administered by Austria-Hungary from 1878
- ▰ Ottoman Empire 1878
- *1817* Date of autonomy within Ottoman Empire
- **1878** Date of independence from Ottoman Empire

▲ The lack of trust between the nations of central Europe was demonstrated when Germany first made an alliance with Russia, and then a pact with Italy guaranteeing that country's neutrality if Russia were to attack Germany. The Triple Alliance held until war broke out, when Italy remained neutral and eventually sided with France and the UK.

◄ The Balkans were under Ottoman rule for more than 300 years, but when the power of the Ottomans declined in the 19th century, Austria-Hungary and Russia both saw a chance to extend their empires. Bosnia was annexed by Austria in 1908. When, however, a Bosnian Serb assassinated the Austrian Archduke Ferdinand and the Austrians attempted to crush the Serb nationalists, Russia intervened.

► When war broke out in the Balkans, the system of European alliances ensured that all the major powers became embroiled.

Europe in 1914
Triple Alliance
Triple Entente
Ally of Central Powers 1914
Future ally of Central Powers
Ally of Entente Powers 1914
Future ally of Entente Powers

THE FIRST WORLD WAR 1914–18

The First World War broke out on 28 July 1914 when Austria-Hungary declared war on Serbia, following the assassination of Archduke Ferdinand by a Serbian nationalist. Russia backed Serbia and began mobilising its troops, and Germany swiftly declared war on Russia and France in support of Austria-Hungary. The United Kingdom declared war on 4 August as Germany stated its aim of launching an attack on France through neutral Belgium. Over the following three years more nations from around the world became embroiled, although the main

fighting took place in Europe and the Middle East. Altogether, 32 nations declared war, the majority of them siding with the original Entente Powers (France, UK and Russia). Italy at first remained neutral, despite being allied to Germany, but in 1915, tempted by the promise of Austrian territory, joined the war on the side of the Entente Powers. The USA declared war on Germany in April 1917, following attacks by German submarines on its merchant ships. US troops and ammunition proved decisive in defeating the Germans on the Western Front.

▼ The war in Europe was waged on many fronts. The Germans advanced into Russia and in 1917 the new communist regime there surrendered. In Arabia a British Empire force from India confronted troops of the Ottoman Empire. Fighting took place in Italy between Austria-Hungary and Italy, and also in the Balkans and eastern Europe.

► On the Western Front a German advance in 1914 was repulsed, and from 1915 until 1918 the position of the two sides remained virtually static, despite the loss of millions of lives. A German advance early in 1918 was initially successful, but the Entente Powers drove the Germans back, and they agreed to an armistice on 11 November 1918.

The Western Front

☐	Central Power
■	Entente Power
▨	Neutral country
– – –	Furthest advance by Central Powers 1914
·········	Furthest advance by Central Powers 1918
–·–·–	Siegfried Line March 1917
▬▬	Area of trench warfare
——	Armistice line 11 November 1918
⊗	Battle won by Central Powers
⊛	Battle won by Entente Powers
✕	Indecisive battle
Arras	Name and year of battle
⌐1914	Marne offensive
▷	The Schlieffen Plan

The War in Europe and the Middle East

——	Borders in 1914
☐	Central Powers
⌐1915⌐	Neutral state that joined Central Powers, with date
■	Entente Powers (including colonies)
⌐1914⌐	Neutral state that joined Entente Powers, with date
▨	Country that remained neutral
——	Furthest advance by Central Powers on date marked

■	Furthest advance by Entente Powers on date marked
⊗	Battle won by Central Powers
⊛	Battle won by Entente Powers
✕	Indecisive battle
↕	Naval engagement
⟹	Allied convoy routes
– – –	Naval blockade of Central Powers

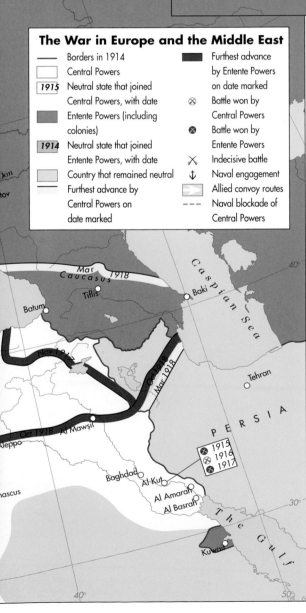

Trench Warfare: Battle of the Somme 1916

⌐⌐	Buildings	⟶	Second British attack, evening 1 July 1916
⟶	First British attack, noon 1 July 1916		
✸	British troops holding out in German trenches		0 metres 500

▲ At the end of 1914 the two sides dug a network of trenches, sometimes only 200 metres apart, in which the soldiers ate and slept.

Shells were fired across 'no-man's-land' into the trenches; soldiers climbing out of a trench were likely to be machine-gunned.

The British launched an attack in the Somme area on 1 July 1916, and on the first day alone over 20,000 British soldiers died.

OUTCOMES OF THE FIRST WORLD WAR

Two months after the armistice of November 1918, the leaders of the victorious Entente Powers (France, the United Kingdom, Italy, the United States and Japan) met at the Paris Peace Conference. Here they decided on the principles that should govern the peace treaties to be made with the defeated Central Powers (Germany,

Austria-Hungary, the Ottoman Empire, Bulgaria and Hungary). Russia, an original member of the Entente when still under tsarist rule, had already made peace with Germany in the Treaty of Brest-Litovsk of March 1918. This had followed the Bolshevik Revolution of October 1917, during which the tsar had been overthrown.

▼ From 1918 to 1920 Bolshevik (communist) Russia was attacked by the tsarist White Russian army and foreign troops. Poland used the opportunity to gain territory from Russia on its eastern border.

The Russian Revolution and Civil War 1917–20

– – – Boundary of the Russian Empire 1914

——— German occupation line March 1918

⟶ White Russian and interventionist attacks

Interventionists:

C Canadian   **F** French

G Greek   **B** British

US American

☐ Area controlled by Bolsheviks October 1919

——— Polish advance into Russia May 1920

——— Russian advance into Poland August 1920

– – – USSR-Polish boundary established October 1920 by Treaty of Riga

——— Other international boundaries 1922

☐ Areas lost to Russia 1914–21

Treaty Settlements in Europe 1919–23

- ——— Boundary 1926
- – – – Pre-war boundary
- ■ Territory administered by League of Nations
- ▨ Demilitarised zone
- **1918** Date of independence
- ——— Internationalised river

Europe in 1914

- ☐ Russian Empire
- ▨ Austro-Hungarian Empire

The Division of the Ottoman Empire

- ▨ Republic of Turkey after Treaty of Lausanne 1923
- ——— Boundary of Turkey after Treaty of Sèvres 1920
- –·–· Boundary of spheres of influence in Turkey 1920–22
- ▨ French mandate
- ☐ British mandate
- ▨ British colony
- ▨ British influence
- *1920* Date of mandate
- **1922** Date of independence

▲ The peace treaties made following the war radically altered the map of Europe. Under the Treaty of Versailles, Germany was considerably reduced in size, losing territory to Poland in the east and to France in the west. A 'buffer zone' was created along the Rhine, from which German troops were prohibited. The Treaty of Saint-Germain broke up the empire of Austria-Hungary into smaller national states. The Treaty of Versailles also called for the creation of the League of Nations. It was hoped that the League, which was based in Geneva, with member states from around the world, would enable disputes to be solved peacefully, by negotiation.

◄ Under the Treaty of Sèvres of 1920, the Ottoman Empire was abolished and Anatolia divided into 'spheres of influence'. However, Mustafa Kemal (later known as 'Atatürk', father of Turkey) led a successful uprising that drove out foreign troops. The Treaty of Lausanne of 1923 recognised the modern state of Turkey. In the Middle East, ex-Ottoman territory was divided by the League of Nations into 'mandates'. These allowed European countries to administer a territory, prior to granting it independence.

THE GREAT DEPRESSION

The Great Depression of 1929–33 was the most severe economic crisis of modern times. Millions of people lost their jobs, and many farmers and businesses were bankrupted. Every country – industrial nations and those supplying the raw materials for factories – was affected. The economies of Germany and the United States were the worst hit. The total value of goods produced by their factories was halved, and between a quarter and a third of their industrial labour force was registered as unemployed by 1932. In the United Kingdom businesses and industries also collapsed, and the already high unemployment rate was doubled.

▼ Northeast Europe was especially badly affected by the Depression. The rate of recovery varied, with unemployment reaching its peak in most countries in 1932, but continuing to rise in others until 1934.

The Effect of the Depression in Europe

- Decline in industrial production of over 30%
- Decline in industrial production of up to 30%
- Area of declining economic activity 1929–32
- Area of economic revival 1929–32

Registered unemployed in '000s:
- 1928
- 1932
- 1934

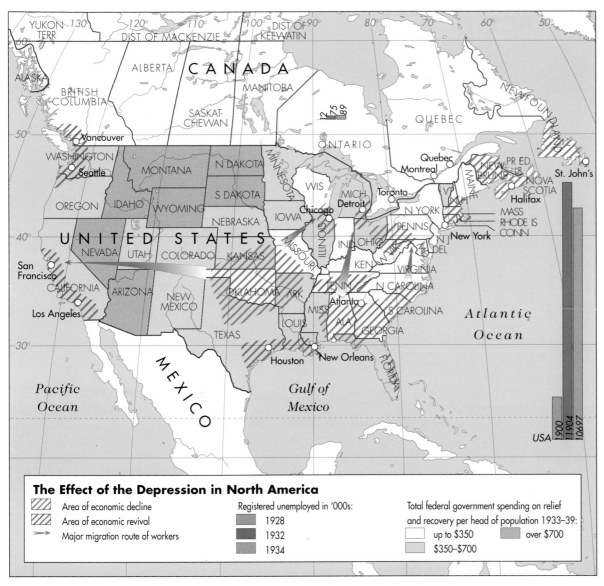

The Effect of the Depression in North America

- ⫽⫽ Area of economic decline
- ⫽⫽ Area of economic revival
- ➔ Major migration route of workers

Registered unemployed in '000s:
- 1928
- 1932
- 1934

Total federal government spending on relief and recovery per head of population 1933–39:
- up to $350
- $350–$700
- over $700

◄ During the 1920s the United States and Canada became increasingly prosperous, but in the Wall Street Crash of October 1929 the value of shares plummeted and millions of investors lost their money. Lack of funds for investment in industry resulted in the value of goods produced declining by 50% in the USA and Canada between 1928 and 1932, thus reducing the amount of money available for reinvestment. In 1930 the Democrat Franklin D. Roosevelt was elected US President. Under his 'New Deal', government money was spent on projects intended to provide employment.

▼ The industries of the USA, Europe and Japan were supplied with raw materials from around the world, so an industrial decline had a global impact. Worst hit were Latin American countries, with China and Malaya also badly affected.

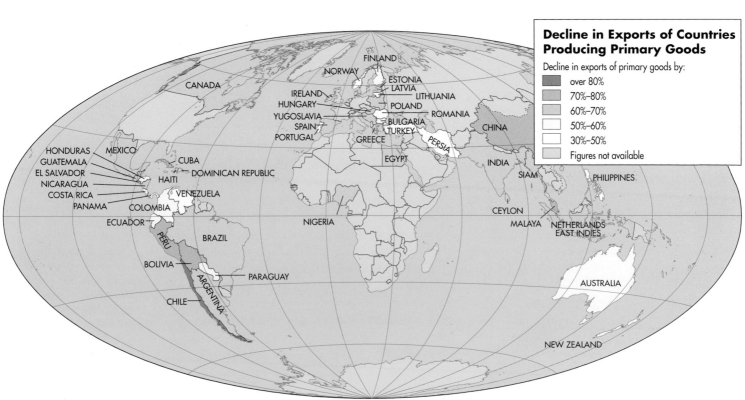

Decline in Exports of Countries Producing Primary Goods

Decline in exports of primary goods by:
- over 80%
- 70%–80%
- 60%–70%
- 50%–60%
- 30%–50%
- Figures not available

THE RISE OF FASCISM

Expansion of Nazi Germany 1933–39

- Germany 1933
- Saarland, incorporated 1935
- Rhineland demilitarized zone, occupied 1936

Territory annexed by Germany:
- on 13 March 1938
- on 1 October 1938
- in March 1939
- by 31 December 1939

Map labels: SWEDEN · DENMARK · Copenhagen · Baltic Sea · LATVIA · Riga · LITHUANIA · Kaunas · Memel Territory 23 March 1939 · Königsberg · EAST PRUSSIA · Danzig 19 Sept 1939 · RUSSIAN OCCUPATION · 17 Sept 1939 · Hamburg · Amsterdam · NETHERLANDS · Weser · Elbe · Berlin · Hanover · Brussels · BELGIUM · Poznan · Vistula · Bug · Warsaw · POLAND · Cologne · Rhine · GERMANY · Leipzig · Odra · GENERAL GOVERNMENT OF POLAND 12 Oct 1939 · LUX · Frankfurt · SUDETEN-LAND · Prague · PROTECTORATE OF BOHEMIA–MORAVIA 16 March 1939 · Krakow · Lvov · SAAR · Saarbrücken · Paris · Seine · Nuremburg · PROTECTORATE OF SLOVAKIA 23 March 1939 · FRANCE · Stuttgart · Rhine · to Hungary 1938 · to Hungary 23 March 1939 · Freiburg · Munich · Danube · Salzburg · Vienna · AUSTRIA · Budapest · HUNGARY · Berne · SWITZERLAND · Innsbruck · Saône · Geneva · Lyons · Trent · ROMANIA · Rhône · Venice · Trieste · ITALY · YUGOSLAVIA · Po

Fascism was a political movement that became popular in Europe during the 1920s and 1930s, a time of extreme hardship for working people. The fascist parties in Italy and Germany attracted supporters by promising to rebuild the economies of their countries, and to provide work for all. During the 1930s the German and Italian governments invested heavily in the manufacture of armaments. They also created jobs in large-scale engineering projects such as the building of roads and power stations.

Mussolini was elected to power in Italy in 1922, but over the next few years he took steps to abolish all political parties apart from the fascists. Adopting the title of 'Il Duce' or 'the leader', he became a dictator. The Nazi Party in Germany, led by Hitler, followed a similar course after Hitler became Chancellor in 1933.

Fascist leaders aimed to unite people from all sections of society – agricultural and industrial workers, the middle-classes and the land- and factory-owners – and to encourage them to think of their nation as better than any other. This unity came at a price, however. The Nazi Party, under Hitler, saw the Germans as a super-race, and excluded from society people whom they considered physically or mentally 'defective'. Jewish people were blamed for Germany's economic problems: their businesses were ruined and they were attacked and imprisoned.

▲ One of Hitler's priorities was to regain territory lost to Germany after the First World War and to unite all German-speaking people. In 1938 Germany annexed Austria and, following the signing of the Munich Agreement with the UK and France, the Sudetenland. German troops took control of the rest of Czechoslovakia in March 1939 and their attack on Poland in September 1939 caused the outbreak of the Second World War.

Right-wing Dictatorships 1919–39

Nazi Germany

Fascist Italy

Other countries under right-wing dictatorships

◀ Fascism developed in its most extreme form in Germany and Italy, but right-wing dictators (who adopted some of the principles of Fascism) came to power across Europe. Czechoslovakia stood out as a beacon of democracy in central Europe.

▼ The Spanish Civil War started in 1936 when an army led by General Franco (the Nationalists) invaded Spain from Morocco, to oust the democratically elected Popular Front government led by Azaña (the Republicans). With military help from fascist Italy and Germany, both of which used the war to test their latest weapons, Franco's army defeated the Republicans in April 1939. Franco then established a dictatorship that was to last until 1975.

Expansion of Italy 1922–39

Italian possessions by 1922

Italian acquisitions 1922–39

1912 Date of acquisition

▲ Mussolini sought to revive Italian national pride and to increase his own personal power by extending Italy's territory on the Adriatic and enlarging its African empire. His invasion of Ethiopia provoked outrage from countries worldwide.

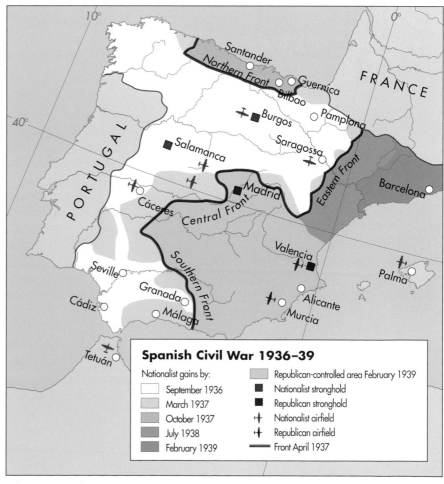

Spanish Civil War 1936–39

Nationalist gains by:

September 1936

March 1937

October 1937

July 1938

February 1939

Republican-controlled area February 1939

Nationalist stronghold

Republican stronghold

Nationalist airfield

Republican airfield

Front April 1937

THE SECOND WORLD WAR IN EUROPE 1939–45

Germany's 'New Order' in Europe November 1942

- German Reich
- Territory under German administration
- Territory under German occupation
- Italy and annexed/administered territories
- Countries co-operating with Axis
- Countries occupied by Axis
- Vichy-governed France
- Unconquered territory of USSR
- Territory of Allied Powers
- Neutral countries
- —— International boundary
- —— German border 1937
- ☒ Concentration camp
- ☒ Death camp

Central Europe 1945

- Future Soviet bloc countries
- Western allies and countries liberated by them
- Neutral countries
- Germany
- Areas controlled by USSR
- Areas controlled by Western allies
- —— Meeting of Soviet and Western forces
- —— International boundary 1945
- • City with four occupation zones

▶ The German invasion of Western Europe in 1940 left the UK vulnerable to attack, although it put up a successful air defence in the Battle of Britain (1940–41). In 1941 Hitler attacked the USSR, but after meeting with initial success, the Germans were forced to retreat in the winter of 1942. At the same time, Allied forces in North Africa defeated Italian and German troops. In 1943 the British and Americans went on the offensive, landing in southern Italy and, in June 1944, in northern France. Allied forces from west and east met in central Germany in May 1945.

◀ By the end of 1942 Germany controlled most of Europe, directly or indirectly, including the puppet-regime of Vichy France. Hitler's 'final solution' was put into effect as Jews and others considered 'undesirable' were transported from all over Europe to death and concentration camps.

War broke out in Europe on 3 September 1939, following Germany's invasion of Poland. France and the United Kingdom were allied against Germany and Italy, which, together with Japan, formed the Axis Powers. Following Germany's successful invasion of the Netherlands, Belgium and France in 1940, the UK remained isolated until the United States joined the war in December 1941. A German invasion of the Soviet Union in 1941 was at first successful, but foundered in the winter of 1942–43. Following the landing of Allied forces on Italian soil, the Italians surrendered in September 1943 and declared war on Germany. German troops continued to put up a strong defence in Italy, on the Eastern Front and against the Allied force that landed in France in 1944, but the Allies eventually forced a German surrender on 7 May 1945.

▶ At the end of the war, Germany and Austria were each divided into four 'zones of occupation', controlled by the Western allies (the UK, the USA and France) and the USSR. The cities of Berlin and Vienna were also divided into four zones. The USSR withdrew from Austria in 1955, but retained indirect control over its German sector until 1989.

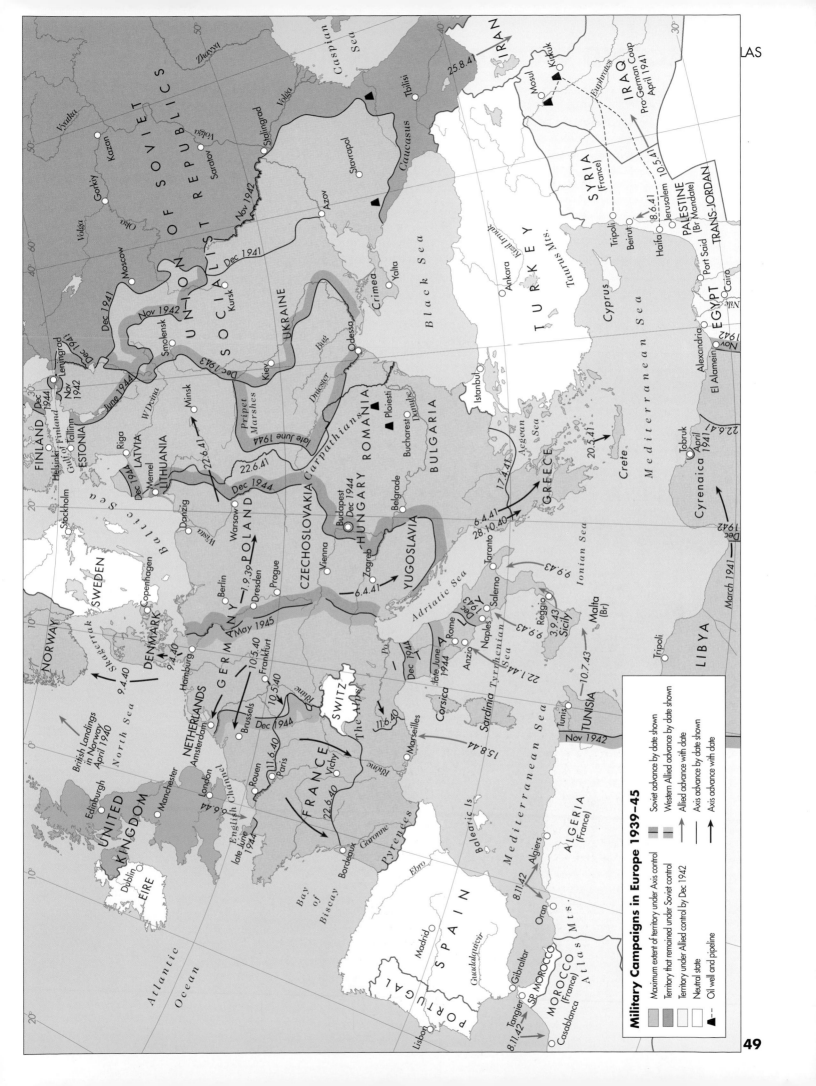

Military Campaigns in Europe 1939–45

THE SECOND WORLD WAR IN ASIA

The war in Asia arose following Japanese incursions into China during the 1930s. Allied with Germany and Italy since September 1940, and threatened with an oil embargo, the Japanese launched a pre-emptive strike against the US fleet in Pearl Harbour, Hawaii, in December 1941. At the same time, they attacked the British in Hong Kong and Dutch territories in Malaysia. For the next six months the Japanese swept through Southeast Asia, but following a surprise defeat by the US navy at the Battle of Midway in June 1942 the tide began to turn. Slowly the US forces, assisted by those from Australia and New Zealand, pushed the Japanese back, while UK and Indian troops defended India. Fighting continued into 1945, with the USA launching bombing raids on Japan. When the Japanese did not surrender, however, the USA decided to use the newly developed atomic bomb. The first bomb was dropped on Hiroshima on 6 August, killing or injuring 130,000 civilians. The dropping of a second bomb on Nagasaki led to the Japanese surrender on 15 August 1945.

▼ The rate of the Japanese advance took the Allied forces by surprise. UK, Dutch and US territories fell like dominoes. French Indochina, under the Vichy government, was sympathetic to Japan, as was Thailand. Japan ruled over its new territories with an iron fist and engaged in atrocities against the native populations and European prisoners of war.

The Japanese Offensive 1941–42

- Japanese Empire 1 Dec 1941
- Thailand, ally of Japan
- Area ceded to Thailand
- Furthest line of Japanese advance July 1942
- 4.42 Month and year of Japanese attack or capture
- ➤➤ Japanese offensive
- ⬱ Japanese naval victory
- ⬰ US naval victory
- ✵ Massacre of civilians
- ⊠ Biological warfare establishment
- ⊠ Site of major war crime

Arctic Ocean

UNION OF SOVIET SOCIALIST REPUBLICS

MONGOLIA

Harbin

MANCHUKUO

Vladivostok

CHINA

Beijing

KOREA

JAPAN

Qingdao

Tokyo

Nanjing 1937

Shanghai

Pacific Ocean

Aleutian Is 6.42

Battle of Midway 6.42

Pearl Harbour 12.41

INDIA

of Cancer

Mandalay 5.42

BURMA

Burma Railway construction

Rangoon 3.42

Guangzhou

Hanoi

Taiwan

Hong Kong 12.41

Hainan

FRENCH INDOCHINA

SIAM (THAILAND)

Bangkok

Saigon

Manila 1945

Manila 1.42

Corregidor 5.42

Bataan Death March

PHILIPPINES

Davao 12.41

Wake Is 12.41

Marshall Islands

Mariana Islands

Guam 12.41

Caroline Islands

attack off Ceylon .42

Kota Bharu 12.41

Miri 12.41

Sandakan Death March

Kuching 1.42

Borneo

Singapore 2.42

Sumatra

Palembang 2.42

Indian Ocean

Batavia 3.42

Bandung 3.42

Java 3.42

Battle of the Java Sea 2.42

Makassar 2.42

Celebes

Bali 2.42

Amboina 2.42

Timor 3.42

Hollandia 3.42

New Guinea

Rabaul 1.42

Buna 7.42

Battle of the Coral Sea 5.42

Guadalcanal 6.42

Solomon Islands

New Hebrides

► During the early 1930s Japan took advantage of a lack of strong government in China to invade the northeast of the country. Outright war was declared between the two countries in 1937 and the Japanese continued to gain ground until 1945. They were driven back largely by Chinese communist troops in the south and west, and by the Soviet army in Manchukuo.

▼ It took the Allies over three years to regain territory that had fallen to Japan over a six-month period. Indeed, when Japan surrendered on 15 August 1945, its troops still occupied a large part of Southeast Asia.

Japan and China 1931–45

- Japanese Empire up to Sept 1931
- Japanese Protectorate from 1932 (Rehe 1933)
- Area occupied by Japan by Dec 1941
- Area occupied by Japan Jan 1942–Aug 1945
- ⮞ Direction of Japanese advance
- Shaanxi-Gansu-Ningxia border region under Communist control
- ⮞ Communist offensive against Japanese 1940
- ✕ Soviet-Japanese border clashes
- → Main supply routes from Allies

The Allied Offensive 1942–45

- ----- Japanese defence perimeter Mar 1944
- -- -- Japanese defence perimeter Oct 1944
- —— Japanese defence perimeter Aug 1945
- ⮞ Japanese late offensive
- ⮞ Allied offensive
- ⮞ British offensive
- ⮞ Chinese–US offensive
- ⮞ Chinese offensive
- ⮞ Soviet offensive
- *4.45* Date of Allied attack or capture
- ⊢ US naval victory
- Conventional bombing
- Nuclear bombing

THE COLD WAR

The Cold War was a political and diplomatic conflict in the years 1947–91 between the United States and its capitalist allies within NATO, and the communist Warsaw Pact countries led by the Soviet Union. It took the form of an arms and space race, the provision of economic and military aid to other countries and, occasionally, direct involvement in regional wars. The Cold War reached it height in 1962, when the Cuban missile crisis almost resulted in a third world war. It ended in 1991 with the disintegration of the East European communist governments and of the Soviet Union.

The Iron Curtain

- Countries under influence of USSR
- Non-aligned communist
- Non-communist
- Iron Curtain
- *1947* Date when communist government was established

▲ After the Second World War an 'Iron Curtain' descended across Europe, dividing the communist regimes of Eastern Europe (which in 1955 formed the Warsaw Pact) from the rest of Europe.

▶ The Korean War was the bloodiest confrontation of the Cold War. After the Japanese surrender in 1945, Korea was divided along the 38th parallel. The war began with an attack by the communist north on the pro-Western south, and involved both Chinese and UN (largely US) troops. A ceasefire line held from 1953, with a permanent peace agreement still not reached in 1998.

◀ The Vietnam War began when communist North Vietnamese troops (Vietcong) attempted to overthrow the US-backed southern regime. US troops became heavily involved in 1964–73 to no avail, and in 1975 North and South were reunited under communist control.

The Vietnam War 1959–75

- → Ho Chi Minh trail
- ➤ US invasion of Cambodia 1970
- ✪ Major US base
- ➤ Strikes by US B52 bombs
- ➤ Bombing raids from US 7th fleet
- Areas largely controlled by Vietcong 1973

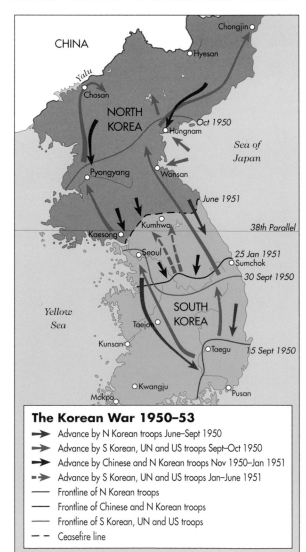

The Korean War 1950–53

- ➤ Advance by N Korean troops June–Sept 1950
- ➤ Advance by S Korean, UN and US troops Sept–Oct 1950
- ➤ Advance by Chinese and N Korean troops Nov 1950–Jan 1951
- ➤ Advance by S Korean, UN and US troops Jan–June 1951
- — Frontline of N Korean troops
- — Frontline of Chinese and N Korean troops
- — Frontline of S Korean, UN and US troops
- -- Ceasefire line

Cold War Conflicts

- Countries in North Atlantic Treaty Organisation (NATO) (1949–)
- Countries in Warsaw Pact (1955–91)
- Non-aligned communist states
- All other countries
- Country with nuclear capability by 1987
- Direct military action by USSR and/or allies
- Direct military action by USA and/or allies
- Economic and political intervention by USSR and/or allies
- Economic and political intervention by USA and/or allies

Conflicts in which the USA, USSR and their allies were involved 1947–91 included:

1. **GREEK CIVIL WAR 1947** USA gave aid to help defeat communists.
2. **BERLIN BLOCKADE 1948–49** USSR attempted to force France, USA and Britain out of West Berlin by imposing a blockade around the city.
3. **FIRST INDOCHINESE WAR 1946–54** French troops tried to prevent independence movement from establishing communism in Vietnam.
4. **KOREAN WAR 1950–53** (See map on opposite page.)
5. **GUATEMALA 1954** USA backed right-wing coup.
6. **HUNGARY 1956** Liberal communist uprising crushed by Soviet troops.
7. **VIETNAM WAR 1959–75** (See map on opposite page.)
8. **SECOND BERLIN CRISIS 1961** East German government erected the Berlin Wall and closed all but one of the access routes to the city. USA sent tanks to Berlin.
9. **CUBAN MISSILE CRISIS 1962** Discovery by USA that USSR was installing nuclear missiles on Cuba resulted in US naval blockade of Cuba and threat of nuclear war. Crisis resolved by USSR agreeing to remove missiles.
10. **DOMINICAN REPUBLIC 1965** USA, fearing communist takeover, sent troops to back government of military junta.
11. **PRAGUE SPRING 1968** Liberal communist government overthrown by troops of USSR and Warsaw Pact allies.
12. **CHILE 1973** USA backed right-wing forces in overthrow of socialist government.
13. **ANGOLA 1974–90** Civil war between MPLA (backed by Soviet-funded Cuban troops) and the FNLA and UNITA (backed by South Africa).
14. **NAMIBIA 1975–91** Communist-backed forces fought for independence of Namibia, illegally incorporated into South Africa.
15. **NICARAGUA 1979** US backing failed to prevent left-wing Sandinistas deposing right-wing regime.
16. **AFGHANISTAN 1979–89** Soviet troops occupied the country to prevent overthrow of pro-USSR regime.

EUROPE AND EUROPEAN EMPIRES SINCE 1945

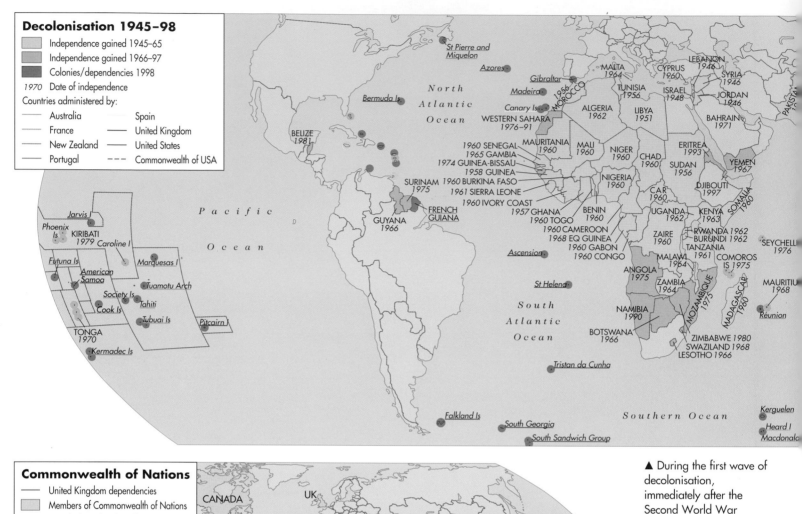

Decolonisation 1945–98

- Independence gained 1945–65
- Independence gained 1966–97
- Colonies/dependencies 1998
- *1970* Date of independence

Countries administered by:
Australia	Spain
France	United Kingdom
New Zealand	United States
Portugal	--- Commonwealth of USA

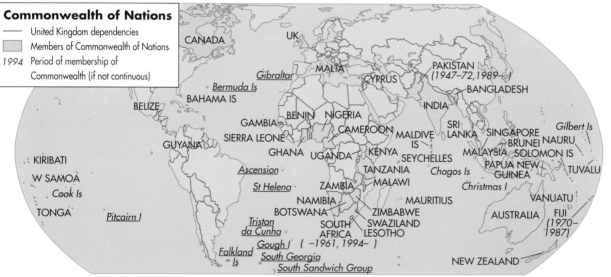

Commonwealth of Nations

- United Kingdom dependencies
- Members of Commonwealth of Nations
- *1994* Period of membership of Commonwealth (if not continuous)

▲ During the first wave of decolonisation, immediately after the Second World War (1939–45), France and Britain gave up their mandates in the Middle East. Independence in Southeast Asia resulted in the formation of the independent states of Malaysia and Indonesia. The French fought against Algerian independence, but gave up their remaining African colonies in 1960. The Portuguese resisted calls for colonial independence until 1974.

▲ The Commonwealth of Nations was founded in 1931 and is an informal organisation, the aim of which is to promote co-operation between Britain and its ex-colonies. The heads of state of the 51 member countries meet every two years to discuss issues of common concern, such as world trade and human rights.

In the period immediately after the Second World War it became clear that the European countries were not going to be able to hold on to their colonial possessions indefinitely. The native inhabitants of colonised countries demanded (and most were eventually granted) the right to govern themselves. At the same time there was a movement towards greater co-operation in Europe, in an attempt to avert another world war. The European Economic Community (EEC) was established in 1957 by the Treaty of Rome.

It aimed to abolish trade barriers between member countries, and to develop a common policy on agriculture. While the EEC (known since 1993 as the European Union) became the main trading block in Western Europe, the communist-controlled states of Eastern Europe formed their own trade organisation, known as COMECON. Since the collapse of communism in Europe and the Soviet Union, many former communist countries have, however, applied to join the European Union.

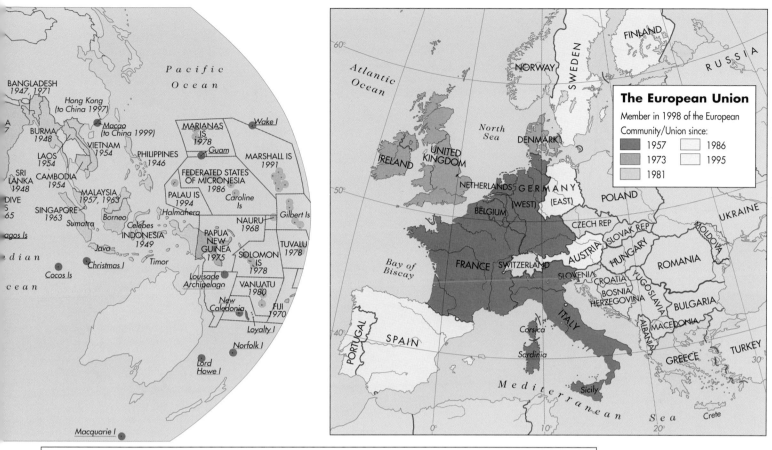

BANGLADESH *1947, 1971*

Hong Kong (to China 1997)

BURMA *1948*
VIETNAM *1954*
LAOS *1954*
PHILIPPINES *1946*

Macao (to China 1999)

MARIANAS IS *1978*
Guam
Wake I

MARSHALL IS *1991*

SRI LANKA *1948*
CAMBODIA *1954*

FEDERATED STATES OF MICRONESIA *1986*

MALAYSIA *1957, 1963*
PALAU IS *1994*
Caroline Is

SINGAPORE *1963*
Borneo
Halmahera
Gilbert Is

Sumatra
Celebes
NAURU *1968*

Java
INDONESIA *1949*
PAPUA NEW GUINEA *1975*
SOLOMON IS *1978*
TUVALU *1978*

Timor

Cocos Is
Christmas I

Louisade Archipelago
VANUATU *1980*

New Caledonia
FIJI *1970*

Loyalty I

Norfolk I

Lord Howe I

Macquarie I

Pacific Ocean
Atlantic Ocean

The European Union

Member in 1998 of the European Community/Union since:

- 1957
- 1973
- 1981
- 1986
- 1995

NORWAY
SWEDEN
FINLAND
RUSSIA
DENMARK
IRELAND
UNITED KINGDOM
North Sea
NETHERLANDS
GERMANY (WEST) (EAST)
POLAND
BELGIUM
CZECH REP
UKRAINE
SLOVAK REP
MOLDOVA
Bay of Biscay
FRANCE
SWITZERLAND
AUSTRIA
HUNGARY
ROMANIA
SLOVENIA
CROATIA
YUGOSLAVIA
BOSNIA HERZEGOVINA
BULGARIA
PORTUGAL
SPAIN
Corsica
ITALY
Sardinia
ALBANIA
MACEDONIA
GREECE
TURKEY
Sicily
Mediterranean Sea
Crete

Break-up of the Soviet Union since 1991

— Border of Soviet Union until 1991
Russian Federation
Constituent republic within Russian Federation
☐ Member state (with Russian Federation) of Commonwealth of Independent States (CIS)
☐ Autonomous area within independent state
State not member of CIS
✿ Area of armed conflict

LATVIA
LITHUANIA
ESTONIA
KARELIA
BELARUS
UKRAINE
Moscow
NENETS
TAYMYR
CHUKCHI
KORYAK
KOMI
MORDVINIA
MARI EL
KOMI-PERMYAK
CHUVASHIA
UDMURTIA
KHANTY-MANSI
YAMAL-NENETS
SAKHA
GEORGIA
KALMYKIA
BASHKORTOSTAN
ADYGEA
KARACHEY-CHERKESSIA
KABARDINO-BALKARIA
NORTH OSSETIA
CHECHENIA, INGUSHETIA
DAGESTAN
RUSSIA
AZERBAIJAN
ARMENIA
TURKMENISTAN
UZBEKISTAN
KAZAKSTAN
KHAKASSIA
UST ORDA BURYATIA
AGA BURYATIA
GORNO-ALTAY
TUVA
EVENK
IRKUTSK
IRAN
KYRGYZSTAN
MONGOLIA
NORTH KOREA
JAPAN
AFGHANISTAN
TAJIKISTAN
CHINA
SOUTH KOREA
PAKISTAN

▲ The European Economic Community originally consisted of six member countries but has expanded substantially over the years. The EEC became the European Community (EC) in 1967. Following the ratification of the Treaty of European Union at Maastricht in 1993, the organisation changed its name again to the European Union (EU).

◄ The Union of Soviet Socialist Republics (Soviet Union) broke up into independent states in 1991, following the introduction of multi-party democracy and the demise of the Communist Party. All the states, except those on the Baltic coastline, agreed to join the CIS, intended to promote common trade, economic, foreign and defence policies. In reality, however, there has been little agreement between member nations, the largest of which is Russia.

ASIA SINCE 1920

Until 1941 India and Southeast Asia were almost entirely under European rule. This situation was shattered, however, by the Japanese invasion of Southeast Asia from December 1941. When the European powers returned, following the defeat of the Japanese in 1945, they found their former colonies determined to rule themselves. The process of establishing independence took over 30 years and involved bloody conflict in Vietnam. The British government bowed to pressure for independence in India in 1947 but, because of religious conflict, divided it into Hindu India and Muslim Pakistan. Following the withdrawal of the colonial powers in Southeast Asia, most of the small states grouped together to form Malaysia (1957) and the Republic of Indonesia (1949). East Timor, made independent from Portugal in 1976, was incorporated by force into Indonesia.

Civil War in China 1945–49
- Area controlled by Communists 1946
- Additional area controlled by Communists June 1949
- Additional area controlled by Communists 1950
- Communist guerrilla operations 1945–49
- Area controlled by Nationalists after 1950
- ✕ Battle with month and year
- ➤ Final Communist campaigns to expel Nationalist armies

◄ The Japanese were expelled from northeast China largely by the USSR. They handed control to the Chinese Communists, who defeated the Nationalists elsewhere in the country, establishing the People's Republic in October 1949.

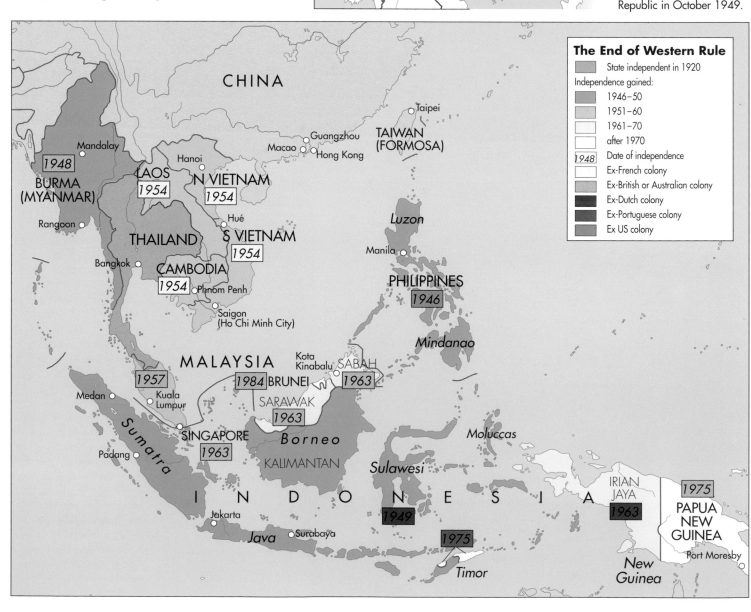

The End of Western Rule
- State independent in 1920

Independence gained:
- 1946–50
- 1951–60
- 1961–70
- after 1970
- *1948* Date of independence
- Ex-French colony
- Ex-British or Australian colony
- Ex-Dutch colony
- Ex-Portuguese colony
- Ex US colony

CHINA

AFGHANISTAN

NW FRONTIER PROVINCE

KASHMIR & JAMMU

TIBET

Lahore
Amritsar
PUNJAB

1

BALUCHISTAN

1

UNITED PROVINCES

BHUTAN

NEPAL

SIKKIM

Delhi

1

RAJPUTANA

Lucknow

ASSAM

AJMER MERWARA

Allahabad

BENGAL

SIND

2

3

BIHAR & ORISSA

Dacca

Karachi

2

Arabian
Sea

WESTERN INDIA STATES AGENCY

4

Ahmedabad

3 2 2 3

Calcutta

4

2

CENTRAL PROVINCES & BERAR

BURMA

4

Nagpur

4

Bombay

Bay of
Bengal

HYDERABAD

BOMBAY

Hyderabad

GOA

MADRAS

Andaman Is

MYSORE

Madras

Administrative Structure of India in the 1930s

Provinces under British rule

States under Indian administration

1 Punjab States Agency

2 Gwalior

3 Central India Agency

4 Baroda

MA Provinces in which Congress party won power in 1937 elections

TRAVANCORE

Nicobar Is

CEYLON

▲ Under British rule, India (with a population of 338 million) was split into administrative regions, some of which were ruled by Indian princes, others by British governors.

◄ After independence Thailand, Malaysia, Singapore, Indonesia and the Philippines set about developing modern industrial economies. With investment from foreign banks and multinational companies, they produced a range of manufactured goods. The industrialisation may have been too rapid, however, for in the late 1990s an economic slump and banking crisis led to social unrest in the region.

AFGHANISTAN

0.7m

Rawalpindi

Lahore

Amritsar

WEST PAKISTAN

4.1m

Delhi

NEPAL

BHUTAN

5.9m

Lucknow

Benares

Allahabad

0.3m

1.2m

Karachi

0.7m

1.0m

Ahmadabad

3.3m

Dacca

Arabian
Sea

I N D I A

Calcutta

EAST PAKISTAN

BURMA

Nagpur

Bombay

HYDERABAD
acceded to
India 1948

Hyderabad

Bay of
Bengal

GOA

Bangalore

Madras

The Partition of India 1947

Muslims as % of total population:

Over 60%   20%–40%

40%–60%   0%–20%

Boundary between India and Pakistan 14 Aug 1947

Muslim refugees to Pakistan

Hindu refugees to India

CEYLON

◄ At the point at which India gained independence in 1947, the sizeable Muslim minority population was given the state of Pakistan (west and east). Seeking safety from religious persecution, millions fled: Hindus into India, and Muslims into Pakistan. East Pakistan gained independence in 1971 to form Bangladesh.

THE MIDDLE EAST AND AFRICA SINCE 1945

Before the Second World War the European powers dominated the Middle East and Africa. In the Middle East they gave up control immediately after the Second World War, but the process of independence in Africa was more gradual. While disputes over territory between newly formed African states have been relatively infrequent, the Middle East has seen several major territorial conflicts: between Israeli Jews and Arab states, Iran and Iraq, and between Iraq and an alliance of Western and Arab states.

▼ The presence of vast oil reserves around the Persian Gulf has enriched the economies of the states that border it and created huge personal fortunes for their ruling families. The Middle East is home to a number of ethnic groups, with Islam the predominant religion.

▶ Israel was founded in 1947 as a homeland for Jews, who for centuries had been dispersed around Europe and America. The new state displaced the Palestinian Arabs, and has thus aroused continual opposition from its Arab neighbours.

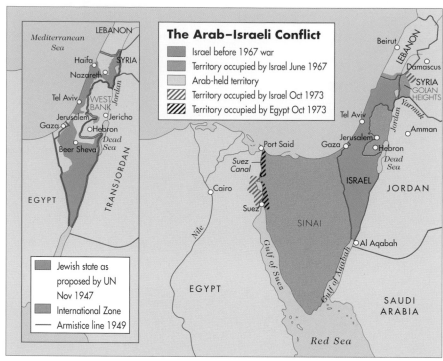

The Arab–Israeli Conflict

- Israel before 1967 war
- Territory occupied by Israel June 1967
- Arab-held territory
- Territory occupied by Israel Oct 1973
- Territory occupied by Egypt Oct 1973

- Jewish state as proposed by UN Nov 1947
- International Zone
- Armistice line 1949

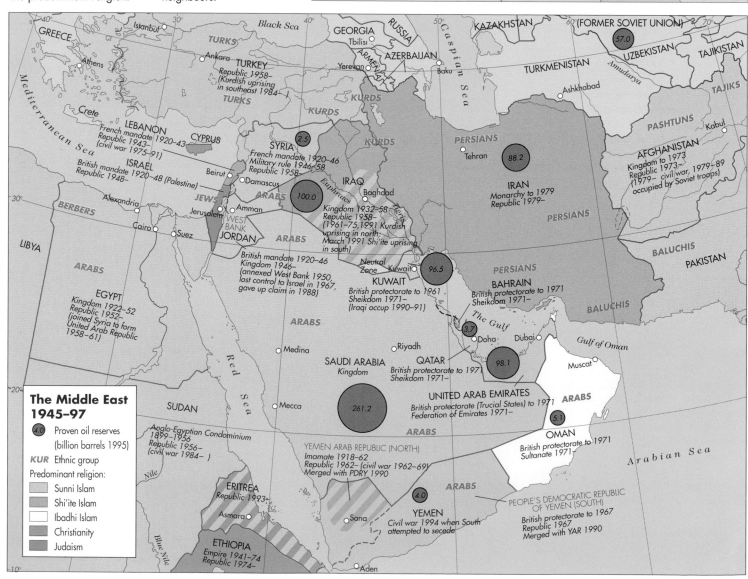

The Middle East 1945–97

- (4.0) Proven oil reserves (billion barrels 1995)
- *KUR* Ethnic group

Predominant religion:
- Sunni Islam
- Shi'ite Islam
- Ibadhi Islam
- Christianity
- Judaism

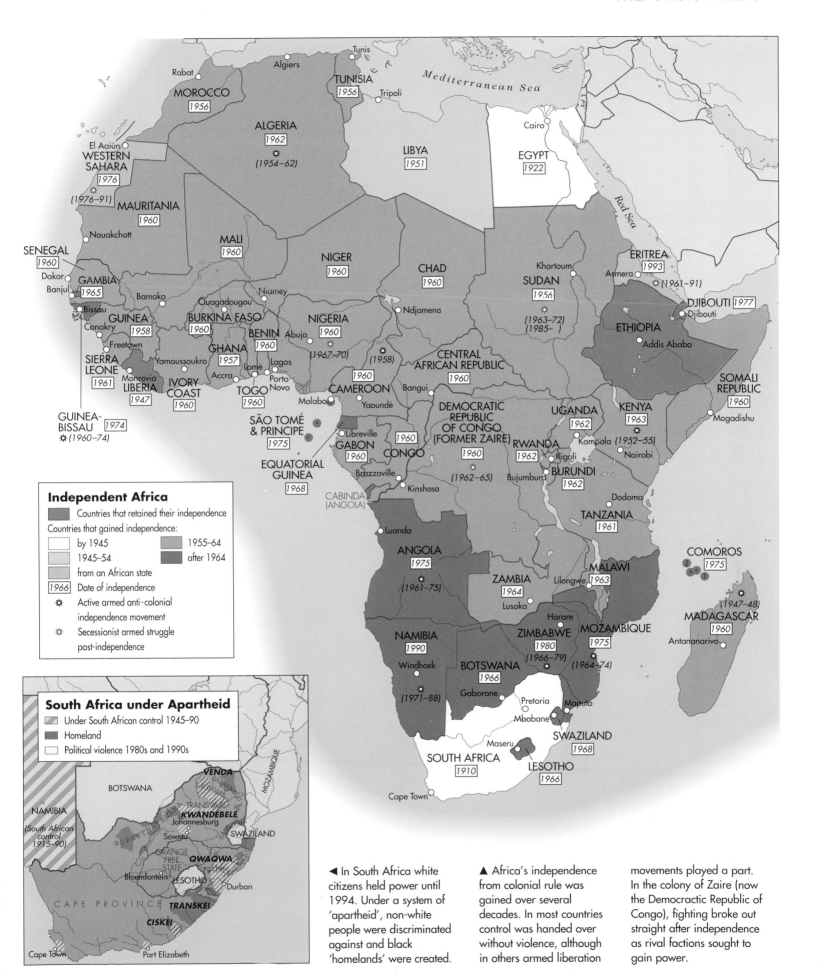

Tunis

Rabat

Algiers

Tripoli

Cairo

Mediterranean Sea

Red Sea

MOROCCO
1956

TUNISIA
1956

ALGERIA
1962
☼
(1954–62)

LIBYA
1951

EGYPT
1922

WESTERN
SAHARA
1976
☼
(1976–91)

El Aaiún

MAURITANIA
1960

Nouakchott

SENEGAL
1960

Dakar

GAMBIA
1965

Banjul

Bissau

Conakry

GUINEA
1958

Freetown

SIERRA
LEONE
1961

Monrovia

LIBERIA
1947

MALI
1960

Bamako

Ouagadougou

BURKINA FASO
1960

Niamey

NIGER
1960

CHAD
1960

Ndjamena

Khartoum

SUDAN
1956

(1963–72)
(1985–)

ERITREA
1993
☼ (1961–91)

Asmera

DJIBOUTI 1977

Djibouti

ETHIOPIA

Addis Ababa

GHANA
1957

Yamoussoukro

Accra

IVORY
COAST
1960

Lomé

TOGO
1960

BENIN
1960

Porto
Novo

Lagos

Abuja

NIGERIA
1960
☼
(1967–70)

☼
(1958)

CAMEROON
1960

Yaoundé

Bangui

CENTRAL
AFRICAN REPUBLIC
1960

UGANDA
1962

Kampala
(1952–55)

KENYA
1963
☼

Nairobi

SOMALI
REPUBLIC
1960

Mogadishu

GUINEA-
BISSAU   1974
☼ (1960–74)

SÃO TOMÉ
& PRINCIPE
1975

Malabo

Libreville

GABON
1960

EQUATORIAL
GUINEA
1968

CONGO
1960

Brazzaville

Kinshasa

CABINDA
(ANGOLA)

DEMOCRATIC
REPUBLIC
OF CONGO
(FORMER ZAIRE)
1960
☼
(1962–65)

RWANDA
1962

Kigali

BURUNDI
1962

Bujumbura

Dodoma

TANZANIA
1961

Luanda

ANGOLA
1975
☼
(1961–75)

ZAMBIA
1964

Lusaka

MALAWI
1963

Lilongwe

Harare

ZIMBABWE
1980
(1966–79)
☼

MOZAMBIQUE
1975
☼
(1964–74)

Maputo

COMOROS
1975

(1947–48)
☼

MADAGASCAR
1960

Antananarivo

NAMIBIA
1990

Windhoek

(1971–88)
☼

BOTSWANA
1966

Gaborone

Pretoria

Mbabane

SWAZILAND
1968

Maseru

LESOTHO
1966

SOUTH AFRICA
1910

Cape Town

Independent Africa

Countries that retained their independence

Countries that gained independence:

by 1945

1945–54

1955–64

after 1964

from an African state

1966   Date of independence

☼   Active armed anti-colonial
independence movement

☼   Secessionist armed struggle
post-independence

South Africa under Apartheid

Under South African control 1945–90

Homeland

Political violence 1980s and 1990s

VENDA

BOTSWANA

GAZANKULU

KWANDEBELE

TRANSVAAL

MOZAMBIQUE

NAMIBIA
(South African
control
1915–90)

Johannesburg

Soweto

SWAZILAND

BOPHUTHATSWANA

ORANGE
FREE
STATE

QWAQWA

Bloemfontein

LESOTHO

Durban

KWAZULU

CAPE PROVINCE

TRANSKEI

CISKEI

Cape Town

Port Elizabeth

◄ In South Africa white
citizens held power until
1994. Under a system of
'apartheid', non-white
people were discriminated
against and black
'homelands' were created.

▲ Africa's independence
from colonial rule was
gained over several
decades. In most countries
control was handed over
without violence, although
in others armed liberation

movements played a part.
In the colony of Zaire (now
the Democractic Republic of
Congo), fighting broke out
straight after independence
as rival factions sought to
gain power.

CO-OPERATION AND CONFLICT

Although the period since the Second World War (1939–45) has seemed relatively calm, with the major powers largely avoiding open conflict, in reality war has been waged almost constantly around the world. Some conflicts, such as that between Iran and Iraq in the 1980s, have been between neighbouring states anxious to expand their territory. Others, such as the conflict in Bosnia in the 1990s, have been 'civil wars', with people of the same country fighting for control. The United Nations, founded in 1945, has attempted to keep the peace in around 40 locations worldwide. Member countries have supplied troops, of whom around 750 were killed in action in the first 50 years of operations.

▼ The UN has become involved in peacekeeping operations when one country has invaded another, as in the Middle East, and in countries suffering civil unrest and conflict, as is the case with UN peacekeeping missions to Somalia and Rwanda in the 1990s.

▶ Discrimination against the Catholic minority in Northern Ireland by the Protestant-controlled regional government led, from 1968 onwards, to conflict between paramilitary groups from both sides of the religious divide, and the deployment of the British army.

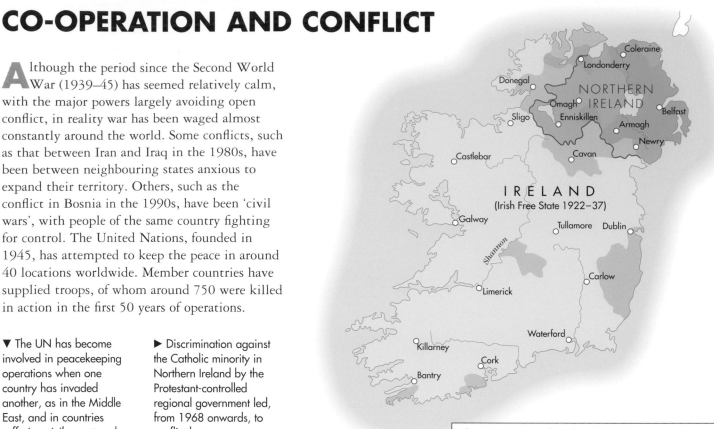

IRELAND
(Irish Free State 1922–37)

The Division of Ireland 1922

—— Boundary between Northern Ireland and Irish Free State, established Dec 1922

Percentage of Protestants:
0–10
10–30
30–50
over 50

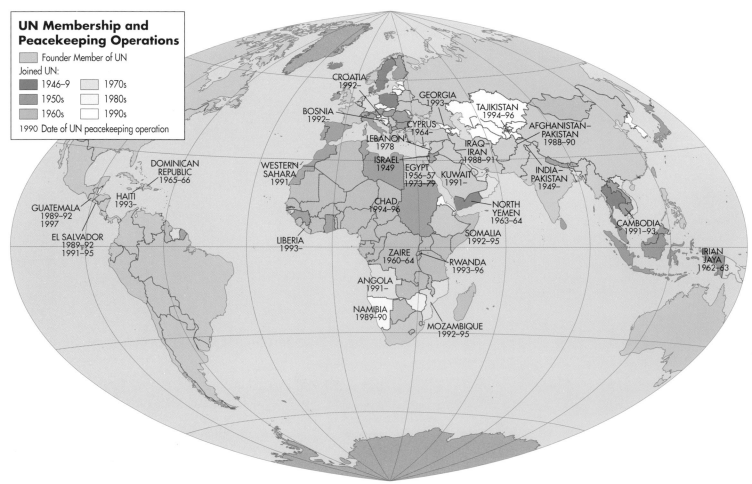

UN Membership and Peacekeeping Operations

Founder Member of UN

Joined UN:
1946–9
1950s
1960s
1970s
1980s
1990s

1990 Date of UN peacekeeping operation

The UN in Bosnia 1994

▦ Area of Bosnia and Croatia controlled by Serbs	◎ UN Safe Area established April 1993
▦ Area of Bosnia controlled by Bosnian Croats	— Boundaries of Bosnia and Croatia
▦ Area controlled by Bosnian Muslims	— Border of former Yugoslavia

The Dayton Peace Agreement 1995

— Dayton Peace Agreement boundary

▦ Muslim–Croat Federation

▦ Bosnian–Serb Federation

▲ Following the collapse of communist rule in 1990, the regions of Slovenia and Croatia both gained independence through armed struggle. Bosnia-Herzegovina, a multi-ethnic area, was torn apart by conflict in 1991–95, as the Bosnian Serbs resisted attempts by the Bosnian Muslims to break away from the control of the Serbian government. The UN failed to bring about peace, which was finally achieved, following NATO direct action, by a team of negotiators at Dayton, Ohio in 1995.

▶ Two wars have arisen since 1980 from Iraq's desire for more oil. The Iran–Iraq War resulted in a ceasefire line little different from the original boundary between the two countries. The Gulf War arose when Iraq invaded oil-rich Kuwait. With the West's oil supplies under threat, a military coalition of the USA, UK, France, Syria, Egypt and Saudia Arabia successfully drove the Iraqis out of Kuwait.

The Gulf Wars 1980–88 and 1990–91

● Oil field

Iran-Iraq War 1980–88:

— furthest points of Iraqi penetration into Iran 1980–82

— furthest points of Iranian penetration into Iraq 1984–87

Gulf War 1990–91:

➤ Iraqi invasion of Kuwait

➤ Allied ground forces counter-offensive

Kurds:

▨ Kurdish region

➤ flight of Kurdish refugees

--- Southern limit of Iraqi 'no-fly zone' from 1991

INDEX

Main entries for subjects are shown in **bold** type.

INDEX